EAT SO

COMPLETE EDITION

Eat So What!
Smart Ways to Stay Healthy

+

Eat So What!
The Power of Vegetarianism

Nutrition Guide for Weight Loss, Disease Free,
Drug Free, Healthy Long Life

LA FONCEUR

CONTENTS

PREFACE

Being a Lacto Vegetarian I always look for the healthy vegetarian options to include in my diet. Everyone's body is different, it reacts differently to food. Some are allergic to nuts, some have a naturally weak immune system. In *Eat So What! Complete Edition*, I have included food options that everyone can include in their diet.

I see various diets trends catching fire every day but these are far from healthy diets, they may give a temporary solution for health issues whether it is obesity, diabetes or other diseases but for a healthy life one must have a thorough knowledge of food that they eat, what is the actual purpose of food and how actually nutritious they are. With *Eat So What! Complete Edition*, I am trying to help people to understand their food in a scientific and real way. This book explains the nutritional value of food, gives direction on what to eat and gives smart tricks and tips to make life healthier. It also explains how you can eat everything provided you follow some simple rules.

Whether you are vegetarian since birth or practicing vegetarianism for health issues or a non-vegetarian, *Eat So What! Complete Edition* book is for you.

Being a Research Scientist and Registered State Pharmacist, I have worked closely with drugs and based on my experience I would suggest not to depend on drugs rather eat healthy vegetarian foods that have the power to prevent you from many diseases, it adds valuable and healthy years to your life. In this book, I am throwing light to the fact that how plant-based healthy vegetarian foods are the remedy to most of your daily health problems.

La Fonceur

BOOK 1

Eat So What!
Smart Ways to Stay Healthy

1. 10 REASONS YOU SHOULD START EATING ALMONDS EVERY DAY

10 Reasons You Should Start Eating Almonds Every Day

Almonds are among the healthiest of tree nuts. Natural, unsalted almonds are a nutritious snack loaded with minerals with plenty of health benefits. Just a handful of almonds (10-15 kernels) a day helps promote heart health, skin and hair health and prevent weight gain, and it may even help fight diseases like Alzheimer's and diabetes.

Types of almonds:

Bitter: These almonds are used for making (almond) oil, which has multiple benefits.

Sweet: Sweet almonds are edible in nature.

Below are 10 reasons you should start eating almonds every day:

1. Almonds Improve Skin Health

Want to have glowing, healthy skin? Eat almonds! Almonds are a great source of vitamin E and antioxidants, which fight free radicals and reduce inflammation, preserving your skin healthy and young. People with dermatitis problem should eat almonds daily. Antioxidants in almonds can fight the damage produced by UV rays, pollution, and a poor diet on the skin. Almonds fight against aging, malnourished skin and prevent skin cancer.

2. Almonds Maintain a Healthy Brain Function

Almonds are rich in riboflavin and L-carnitine. These two substances prevent cognitive decline and support healthy neurological activity, reducing the inflammatory processes in the brain. Eating almonds on a daily basis can prevent cognitive diseases, like dementia and Alzheimer's disease.

3. Almonds Improve Hair Health

Almonds are absolutely bursting with biotin. A single serving contains over 50 percent of your daily value. Biotin (also known as vitamin H) helps a number of bodily processes, but perhaps its most prominent role is aiding in the formation of healthy hair. Deficiency in biotin can lead to an unhealthy scalp and brittle, thinning hair. Since just a single serving of almonds contains over half your daily requirement, they're a fantastic food for keeping hair strong, healthy and beautiful.

4. Almonds Keep Heart Healthy and Prevent Heart Attacks

Almonds have high levels of monounsaturated and polyunsaturated fats. Also known as "good fats," they have been shown to have a significant positive impact on cholesterol. A better cholesterol profile greatly reduces the risk of blocked arteries, the biggest culprit behind heart attacks and strokes. Eating more almonds equals a healthier heart.

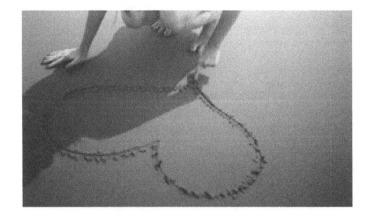

5. Almonds for Weight Loss

Almonds are packed with a lot of fiber, and protein content which takes a longer time to digest, which results in a fuller stomach and lesser cravings. Plus, protein helps in the development of lean muscle mass. Almonds are a perfect low-carb snack and ideal for those who are on a low-carb diet.

6. Almond Benefits Blood Pressure Levels

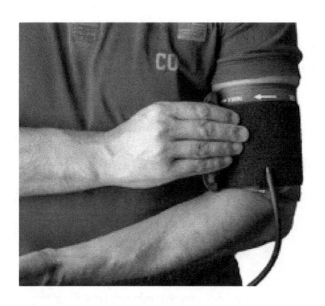

Almonds fend off magnesium deficiency. A deficiency in magnesium is strongly linked to high blood pressure. If you do not meet the dietary recommendations for magnesium, adding almonds to your diet could have a huge impact. The magnesium in almonds may help lower blood pressure levels. High blood pressure is one of the leading drivers of heart attacks, strokes, and kidney failure.

7. Almond Increase Digestion and Metabolism

Almonds are good for digestion. Eating almonds could help improve digestive health by increasing levels of beneficial gut bacteria. As well as being high in vitamin E and other minerals, almonds are now believed to increase good bacteria in the gut. Almond milk contains secret traces of fiber. Fiber is known for its digestion-enhancing benefits. Thus, almond milk eases the problem of indigestion largely. Increased digestion flushes unwanted and unhealthy toxins out of the human body system. This further increases the metabolic rate of the human body.

8. Almonds Prevent Cancer

Almonds are an excellent reserve of vitamin E, phytochemicals, and flavonoids, which control the progression of breast cancer cells. Fibers in almonds help in detoxifying the body. It enables food to move through the digestive system more efficiently. This process cleanses the digestive system, thus lower the risk of colon cancer.

9. Almonds Strengthen Bones and Teeth

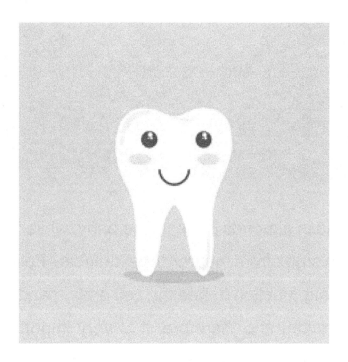

Almonds contain nearly 200 mg of the recommended daily dose of calcium, they also deliver a whole host of nutrients—fiber, manganese, phosphorus, vitamin E, which avert osteoporosis and strengthen teeth and improve bone mineral density and strengthen the skeletal system.

10. Almonds Prevent Birth Defects

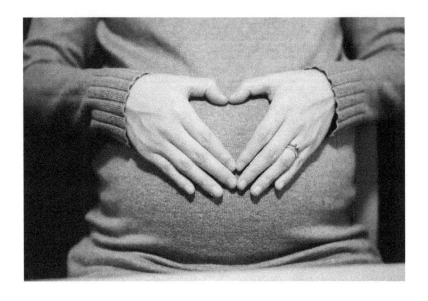

Folic acid in almonds protects the baby, while it is still in the womb, from neural tube defects. Folic acid plays a big function in healthy cell growth and tissue configuration, and therefore, it is very important for the healthy growth of the fetus. It also helps with the development of the nervous system and the bones.

Conclusion

One should eat soaked almonds as soaking almonds neutralize enzyme inhibitors, thus aiding digestion. Soaking almonds help in reducing phytic acids in the outer layer of almonds. The outer layer of bran of almonds can block calcium absorption and also affect the amount of magnesium, iron, copper, and zinc, which we consume. Soaked almonds have higher B Vitamins. They help in the breakdown of gluten, which neutralizes toxins in colons and makes proteins more available for absorption. It is also to be kept in mind that almonds have calories and hence should be consumed in controlled quantities. Excess consumption of almonds can be bad for the heart as well as your body weight.

2. 10 SMART WAYS TO LOSE WEIGHT WITHOUT DIETING

10 Smart Ways to Lose Weight Without Dieting

Diet plans can be challenging to stick to for prolonged periods. Imagine eating whatever you like still not gaining an inch of extra fat. Yes, you read it right! There are other smart ways to lose weight without dieting or exercising. Implement the following tips in your life and maintain your desired weight you always dreamt of. These methods work for everyone and are the best-kept secrets for weight loss.

Read carefully the 10 smart ways to lose weight without dieting:

1. Hold Your Stomach In

When you slightly tucked in your stomach while eating, you eat less. That doesn't mean you force yourself too much, but this trick always works. Wearing form-fitting clothes or wearing an outfit with a waistband serve as a tool to prompt you to slow down and assess how you feel during your meal. Not only while eating but in general hold your stomach in, while sitting before the laptop or watching television, soon it will become a habit.

2. Laugh Out Loud

Laughter is a great antidote to stress. Laughing raises energy expenditure and increases the heart rate of 10 to 20%. Laughter reduces the levels of the stress hormone cortisol, which lowers the metabolism and stores fat in the midsection. This means, laughter will help improve your metabolism naturally, which in turn, influences your body to burn more calories and lose weight.

3. Sleep Well

Sleep is like nutrition for the brain. Most people need between 7 and 9 hours each night. Too little sleep triggers a cortisol spike. This stress hormone signals your body to conserve energy to fuel your waking hours. A lack of sleep may disrupt the appetite-regulating hormones leptin and ghrelin. Having these hormones fluctuate can increase your hunger and cravings for unhealthy food, leading to higher calorie intake. Lack of sleep and stress may increase the risk of several diseases, including obesity and type 2 diabetes.

4. Eat Smaller Portions

You can eat whatever you want, but the secret trick for losing weight is controlling the portion. Larger portions encourage people to eat more and have been linked to an increase in weight gain and obesity. To lose weight, you need to burn more calories than you consume, which inevitably means portion control. When you are eating out, sharing is caring, eat half, or share the meal with a friend.

5. Eat Protein in Breakfast

Protein is important because it helps you feel fuller longer. This is because protein affects several hormones that play a role in hunger and fullness, including ghrelin and GLP-1.

Eating protein in breakfast slows down digestion making you feel more satisfied by increasing feelings of fullness, reduce hunger, and help you eat fewer calories for the rest of the day. Some examples of protein-rich foods include lentils, quinoa, almonds, and Greek yogurt.

6. Take A Walk After Meal

A brief walk shortly after eating is a quick way to burn some calories and aid digestion. A post-meal walk, as short as 15 minutes, can, in fact, help with digestion and improve blood sugar levels, boost your energy, and burn calories. Walking at a brisk speed for 30 minutes as soon as possible just after lunch and dinner leads to more weight loss than does walking for 30 minutes beginning one hour after a meal has been consumed.

7. Add Chili Peppers in Your Diet

Eating chili peppers can help you to lose weight by speeding up your metabolism and burning away fat. Capsaicin, a substance present in peppers, gives them their heat. The heat, which is provided by capsaicin, help your body to convert fat into heat and thus, burns fat, which results in weight loss.

8. Eat Fiber-Rich Foods

Eating fiber-rich foods may increase satiety, helping you feel fuller for longer. Fiber has Flush Effect, which means it helps reduce the absorption of calories from the food you eat. Fiber slows down your body's conversion of carbohydrates to sugar. This helps stabilize blood glucose levels and helps you lose weight. You can eat a lot of fiber-rich food without eating a lot of calories. Some examples of fiber-rich foods include flax seeds, oats, beans, oranges, and Brussels sprouts.

9. Drink Water When You Crave for Snack

Drinking water can help you eat less and lose weight as water is an appetite suppressant. If you feel a sudden urge for a specific food, try drinking a large glass of water and wait a few minutes. Sometimes our body gives a false alarm. Drink at least 8 glasses of 250 ml glass of water in a day. If you replace calorie-loaded drinks — such as soda or juice — with water, you may experience an even greater effect.

10. Eat Slowly and Chew Thoroughly

Your brain needs time to receive the fullness signals. It takes up to 20 minutes for your brain to get the signal that your stomach is full. Eating too quickly often leads to overeating. When you eat slowly, you consume less amount of food. Chewing your food thoroughly makes you eat more slowly. You should chew your food at least 32 times. Chewing your food thoroughly also improves digestion and let you lose weight faster.

Conclusion

A few simple changes in lifestyle can have a massive impact on your weight over a long period of time. The best part of the above tips is that you don't need to give up completely your favorite food. However, adding exercise to these healthful habits can also improve a person's weight loss results. Don't take the burden on yourself by applying all the tips at once. Apply tips one by one, soon it will become your habit, and I bet you will never feel the need to go on a diet again in your life.

3. 10 FIBER RICH FOODS FOR BETTER DIGESTION

10 Fiber Rich Foods for Better Digestion

You should eat more fiber. You've probably heard it before. But why fiber is so good for your health, do you know that? Let's dig deeper into it.

What is Dietary Fiber?

Dietary fiber is the portion of plant-derived food that cannot be completely broken down by digestive enzymes. It passes relatively intact through your stomach, small intestine, and colon and out of your body.

Types of Fiber

Soluble fiber – This type of fiber dissolves in water – is readily fermented in the colon into gases and physiologically active by-products. It is viscous, maybe called prebiotic fiber, and delays gastric emptying which, in humans, can result in an extended the feeling of fullness.

Insoluble fiber – This type of fiber does not dissolve in water – is inert to digestive enzymes in the upper gastrointestinal tract and provides bulk. Bulking fibers absorb water as they move through the digestive system, easing defecation.

How does Fiber help in digestion?

Fiber plays a major role in digestive health. Fiber is the fuel; the colon cells use to keep them healthy. Soluble fiber attaches to cholesterol particles and takes them out of the body, helping to reduce overall cholesterol levels and the risk of heart disease while Insoluble fiber helps to keep the digestive tract flowing, by keeping your bowel movements soft and regular.

Below are the 10 Fiber Rich Foods For Your Better Digestion:

1. Chia Seeds

Chia seeds are tiny black seeds that form a gel when comes in contact with water. They're highly nutritious, containing high amounts of magnesium, phosphorus, and calcium. Chia seeds are very high in fiber.

The fiber in chia seeds absorbs a good amount of water and expands in the stomach, helping to keep you feeling fuller for longer. An amazing source of fiber, protein, and minerals, chia seeds are perfect for decreasing cholesterol, boosting bowel function, and reducing inflammation in the body. Soak chia seeds overnight and eat them in breakfast by adding to your favorite smoothie to get your daily recommended intake of fiber.

2. Oats

Oats are high in vitamins, minerals, and antioxidants. They contain a powerful soluble fiber called oat beta-glucan, which has major beneficial effects on blood sugar and cholesterol levels. Soluble fiber from oatmeal binds with bile acids in your gut, helping excess cholesterol go out through waste, ultimately lowering your cholesterol level. As it goes through the digestive system, it turns into a gel that slows digestion, keeping you feeling fuller longer. Oats increases the growth of good bacteria in the digestive tract.

3. Chickpeas

The chickpea is a type of legume which is loaded with nutrients, including protein and minerals. Chickpeas are rich in prebiotic fibers which act as food for healthy bacteria in your digestive system. This can lead to a reduced risk of some digestive conditions, such as irritable bowel syndrome and colon cancer. Protein and fiber work synergistically to slow digestion, which helps promote fullness. Chickpeas contain soluble fiber; it blends with water and forms a gel-like substance in the digestive tract.

4. Lentils

Lentils are very high in protein and loaded with many important nutrients. Lentils contain both insoluble and soluble fiber. That means they make you full by expanding in the stomach and absorbing water. Additionally, their fiber can help improve heart, digestive immune and metabolic function, by carrying waste, excess fat, and toxins out of the body.

5. Apples

Apples are among the tastiest and most satisfying fruits you can eat. They are also relatively high in fiber. Apples contain a unique type of fiber called pectin, which has been shown to help improve digestion because of its soluble nature and ability to bind to cholesterol or toxins in the body and get rid of them. Due to the high content of fiber, apple makes you feel full; eating an apple a half hour to an hour before a meal has the result of cutting the calories of the meal.

6. Sweet Potatoes

Sweet potatoes are super healthy and have a delicious sweet flavor. They are very high in beta-carotene, B vitamins, and various minerals. They are best had with their skins if you want to benefit your digestive system. With the peel on, their fiber content gets better. The starchy texture of sweet potatoes contains fiber, which aids digestion. They are soothing to the stomach and intestines so you can avoid any difficulties of digesting them.

7. Kidney Beans

Kidney beans are good for digestion. Kidney beans contain both soluble and insoluble fiber, which keep your digestive system running smoothly. Soluble fiber slows down digestion, which gives you that full feeling and insoluble fiber helps prevent constipation. But you have to ensure that you do not overindulge to prevent the problems like gas and flatulence.

8. Brussels Sprouts

The Brussels sprout is a type of cruciferous vegetable that resembles mini cabbages. They are high in vitamin K, folate, potassium, and potent cancer-fighting antioxidants as well as dietary fiber. Eating Brussels sprouts, along with other good sources of fiber like fruits, vegetables, and whole grains can easily help you meet your daily fiber needs.

Brussels sprouts are rich in substances known as glucosinates, which can protect the mucosal lining of the GI tract and reduce the risk of digestive disorders.

9. Carrots

Carrots are high in vitamin K, vitamin B6, magnesium and beta-carotene, an antioxidant that gets turned into vitamin A in the body. Though they are good for the eyes, they are also good for digestion. They are a very good source of fiber and antioxidants and can help you maintain good digestive health.

The soluble fiber in carrots can benefit your digestive organs in many ways, promoting digestion. This fiber is essential to regulating your digestion and also helps to keep cholesterol levels healthy.

10. Avocado

Avocados are among the best sources of fiber in fruits. It is super rich in fiber along with healthy monounsaturated fats and essential nutrients, such as potassium, which helps promote healthy digestive function. Besides, it can help convert beta-carotene into vitamin A. This helps in maintaining a mucosal lining in the gastrointestinal tract, which helps in digestive processes. It's also a low-fructose food, so it's less likely to cause gas. The fiber in avocado can help prevent constipation, maintain a healthy digestive tract, and lower the risk of colon cancer.

Conclusion

Good digestion is key for a good life. By keeping your digestive system healthy, you can keep many diseases at bay. Fiber-rich foods play an important role in digestion by helping food move through your system more easily or quickly. If you're seeking relief for your digestive woes, consider adding fiber-rich foods to your diet. After all, prevention is better than cure.

4. 10 BEST FOODS FOR BETTER SKIN

10 Best Foods for Better Skin

Our life seems to be speeding up and becoming less empathic and increasingly stressful, which put extra stress on our skin health. Our dependence on processed food is increasing day by day. Processed, refined, and manufactured foods and snacks fuel inflammation on the skin. Skin inflammation can cause redness, acne, and wrinkles.

But nature has solution to all the problems. We are blessed with some magic food which protects skin cells from the sun's rays, some keep skin hydrated, and some limit skin damage from harmful molecules known as free radicals and build strong cell walls for smooth and firm skin.

Below are the 10 best foods for better and healthier skin:

1. Almonds

Almonds are a great source of vitamin E and antioxidants, which fight free radicals and reduce inflammation, preserving your skin healthy and young. People with dermatitis problem should eat almonds daily. Antioxidants in almonds can fight the damage produced by UV rays, pollution, and a poor diet on the skin. Almonds fight against aging, malnourished skin and prevent skin cancer.

2. Dark Chocolate

Cocoa beans, from which chocolate is derived, are rich in flavanols, which is a very potent antioxidant which protects skin from UV damage, prevents dark spots, premature aging, rashes, and skin cancer, and boost circulation for a healthy glow.

But be sure to avoid any chocolate less than 70 percent cocoa, like milk chocolate, which contains loads of sugar and dairy, which can be terrible for your skin. Look for high cocoa concentrations for the highest concentration of antioxidants to hydrate your skin and improve circulation, leading to healthier, younger-looking skin.

3. Peppers

Yellow and green peppers are an excellent source of beta-carotene, another antioxidant which your body converts into vitamin A.

Bell peppers are also one of the best sources of vitamin C, necessary for creating the protein collagen which keeps skin firm and strong. Carotenoids decrease sun sensitivity, diminishing the appearance of fine lines around the eyes.

4. Walnuts

Walnuts have both omega-3 and omega-6 fatty acids more than any other nuts; these are the fats that your body cannot make itself.

Omega-3 fatty acids may improve the condition of psoriasis or eczema by reducing the inflammatory compounds in the body.

Walnuts contain zinc, which is necessary for wound healing and combatting both bacteria and inflammation.

Zinc is essential for your skin to function properly as a barrier. Walnuts also provide small amounts of the antioxidants, vitamin C, vitamin E, and selenium, and protein.

5. Tomatoes

Lycopene, is a bright red carotene and carotenoid pigment and phytochemical found in tomatoes, a potent antioxidant to protect skin from UV damage.

They may also help prevent wrinkling.

Tomatoes are also a great source of vitamin C. Fat increases the absorption of carotenoids. Consider pairing carotenoid-rich foods like tomatoes with a source of fat, like olive oil. Add tomato paste in your face pack paste for instantly glowing skin.

6. Green Tea

Green tea may protect your skin from damage and aging. The powerful compounds found in green tea are called catechins, a type of polyphenols making it an antioxidant and an anti-inflammatory which improve the health of your skin in several ways. The vitamin K in green tea helps lighten dark circles under the eyes.

Drinking green tea daily could reduce redness from sun damage. Green tea is great for healing scars and blemishes and flushes out toxins. It also improves the moisture, roughness, thickness, and elasticity of the skin.

Try to avoid adding milk to your tea as milk could

reduce the impact of green tea's antioxidants.

7. Oranges

Oranges are citrus fruits packed with vitamin C, minerals, dietary fiber, which reduces wrinkles and age-related dry skin. Body needs vitamin C to produce collagen, a protein that keeps skin firm and fights the appearance of aging. Vitamin C boosts immunity, thereby protecting the skin from infections and diseases. Oranges have a high content of citric acid, which aids in skin exfoliation and helps to dry out acne, improving the overall look of your skin.

Drinking orange juice regularly increases skin carotenoids an antioxidant which can help protect the skin from harmful radiation, pigmentation, and prevent inflammation. A single medium orange has more than enough of the daily recommended intake of vitamin C.

8. Papayas

Papaya has skin lightening properties that help clear blemishes and pigmentation. The delicious Papayas contain enzymes papain and chymopapain, vitamins A, C, and B, and dietary fiber. Papaya can help lower blood pressure thereby slowing aging. Papaya improves bowel movement and digestion. This, in turn, can help you get fresh and infection-free skin as better digestion means you will be flushing out toxins that can prevent acne and pigmentation.

9. Avocados

Avocados help prevent sun damage, while also strengthening and rejuvenating the skin. Avocados are high in monounsaturated fats and polyunsaturated fats, which are healthy fats. Getting enough of these fats is essential to keep skin flexible and moisturized. These fats benefit many functions in your body, including the health of your skin. Avocados protect skin from oxidative damage caused by the sun, which can lead to signs of aging.

Avocados are rich in vitamins A, E, C, K, B-6, folate, niacin, pantothenic acid, riboflavin, choline, lutein, potassium, and magnesium. Consuming healthy fats is critical as they help maintain cell integrity and aid in healthy aging.

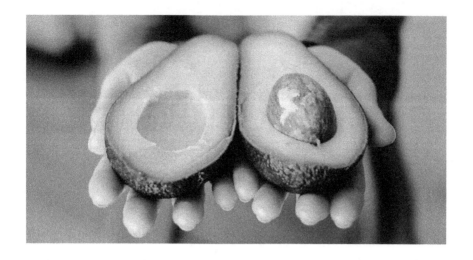

The antioxidants vitamins A and E, which guard against UV rays and keep skin moisturized. Avocados are also a good source of vitamin E, which is an important antioxidant that helps protect your skin from oxidative damage. Skin needs Vitamin C to create collagen, which is the main structural protein that keeps your skin strong and healthy.

10. Olive Oil

Olive oil consists mainly of oleic acid (up to 83%) monounsaturated fatty acids, which may play a role in the youth boost. The antioxidant polyphenols in olive oil help flush out the toxins and could also quench damaging free radicals.

Olive oil is loaded with vitamin E, which acts as an antioxidant that preserves your skin healthy and young. Applying olive oil topically can protect the skin from UV radiation and reduce the risk of skin cancer.

Conclusion

Who doesn't want clean, clear, and supple skin? Foods, as mentioned above, are readily available in the market. It would be a wiser decision to eat these foods instead of spending on cosmetics for better skin. Why go for a temporary solution for your skin when you can have permanent healthy, better-looking skin for life without any fuss. Think again!

5. 10 REASONS WHY ALCOHOL IS A BIG NO NO!!!

10 Reasons Why Alcohol is A Big No No!!!

For many people, alcohol consumption has become a part of life. Alcohol is basically a chemical that can damage the body and may result in death; still drinking is considered socially acceptable in many parts because it is legal. Many people consider alcohol as a stress reliever who want to forget about the worries and tension of the day. However, as per a study, the fact is any amount of alcohol consumption is bad for health. If you still not convinced then read carefully below, the most important reasons you should quit alcohol as early as you can.

Below are the top 10 reasons why alcohol is a big no no:

1. Promotes Depression

Are you worried about why you feel depressed all the time, for every small issue? Alcohol is a direct central nervous system depressant which disrupts mood stability and promotes depression.

2. Brain Disorders

Alcohol interferes with the process of memory and affects the ability of new learning, just one or two drinks can cause blurred vision, slurred speech, slower reaction times, impaired memory, and loss of balance. Short-term effects disappear when the individual stops drinking, but long-term alcohol abuse may cause chronic brain disorders that are serious and debilitating.

3. Cancer

Alcoholic beverages are classified by the International Agency for Research on Cancer (IARC) as a Group 1 carcinogen (carcinogenic to humans). Long-term drinking is associated with a higher risk of certain types of cancer, including cancer of the liver, mouth, throat, larynx (the voice box), esophagus, and breast. Drinkers who also smoke are at a higher risk of developing cancer. 3.6% of all cancer cases and 3.5% of cancer deaths worldwide are attributable to consumption of alcohol (also known formally as ethanol).

4. Weight Gain

Alcohol can cause weight gain in four ways: it stops your body from burning fat, it's high in kilojoules, it can make you feel hungry, and it can lead to poor food choices.

5. Injury

According to the Centers for Disease Control and Prevention, drinking slows reaction time and impairs judgment and coordination. Individuals under the influence of alcohol are more likely to be involved in accidents.

6. Birth Defects

Pregnant women should not drink at all. Exposing the
fetus to alcohol can cause birth defects of the brain,
heart, and other organs. A woman is at risk of giving
birth to a child with fetal alcohol syndrome if she
drinks while pregnant. Fetal alcohol syndrome (FAS)
is a condition that affects the developing fetus.
Children suffering from fetal alcohol syndrome often
have abnormal facial characteristics, stunted growth,
brain damage, organ defects, problems paying

attention, and poor coordination. There is no cure for fetal alcohol syndrome; once the damage is done to a child, he or she must suffer for life.

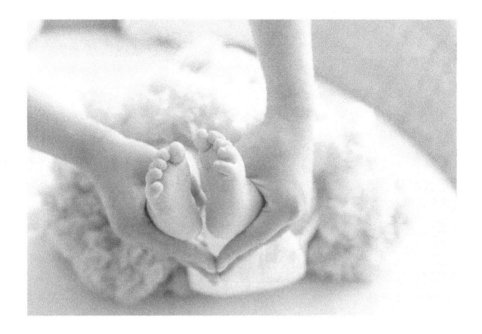

7. Cirrhosis of the Liver

Alcohol can lead to permanent organ damage. Cirrhosis of the liver can be fatal because the damaged liver can no longer perform the essential processes necessary to keep the body functioning optimally. Cirrhosis affects the liver's ability to convert food into energy and prevent the organ from removing toxins from the body. The liver in people with cirrhosis contains scar tissue that reduces the flow of blood through the organ.

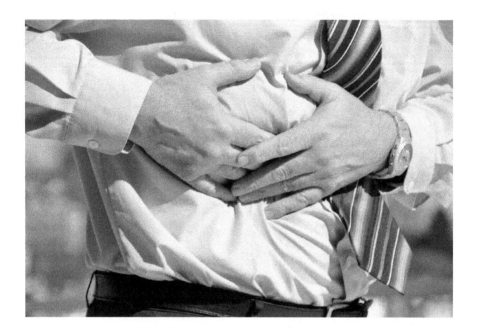

8. Serious Chronic Diseases

According to the Centers for Disease Control and Prevention, drinking alcohol over extended periods of time can cause high blood pressure, liver cirrhosis (damage to liver cells), and pancreatitis (inflammation of the pancreas).

9. Drug Interaction

Alcohol interferes with the therapeutic effects of

prescribed medication, including anti-depressant and anti-anxiety medications. I can be dangerous in combination with other medicines. Never ever take Aspirin for a headache caused by alcohol, it can cause internal gastric bleeding, which can be life-threatening.

10. Abnormal Sleep Pattern

Alcohol interrupts the normal sleep pattern, which affects energy, mood, anxiety level. You feel tired all day.

My Thoughts

It is a misconception that you can only enjoy your life with a glass of alcoholic beverage. Human has a tendency to follow what he sees; it's not completely our mistake as we often see in movies and serials portraying alcohol as a fun factor of life. They portray the most dangerous substance alcohol as a cool thing or as a status symbol, but we should never forget that movies, serials are the pure art of fiction and has nothing to do with real life. I am a scientist, I have closely worked with alcohol, and for me, alcohol is just another chemical substance which we use in a very very minute amount to prepare tablets and capsules to treat a particular disease. We use alcohol in a little amount as we know how dangerous alcohol is for our body. You only live once; it's better to live disease-free, frustration-free, depression-free. It's your fundamental right; don't let alcohol to steal your basic living rights.

6. 10 SMART WAYS TO INCORPORATE PUMPKIN INTO YOUR DIET

10 Smart Ways to Incorporate Pumpkin into Your Diet

When I was a kid, my Mom used to chase me to make me eat pumpkin subji (curry) along with a long lecture on benefits of pumpkin, but as a kid, I was not a fan of pumpkin. Yes, we all have been gone through this. I wish someone had told my Mom the smart ways to incorporate pumpkin in the diet like I am telling you today.

Before going in more detail, let's first see why pumpkin is so important to eat, especially if you are a student.

Benefits of Pumpkin:

- Pumpkin is high in vitamins and minerals while being low in calories as it's 94% water which makes pumpkin a weight-loss friendly food.
- It's also a great source of beta-carotene, a carotenoid that body converts into vitamin A. Vitamin A is essential for eyesight and helps the retina absorb and process light, which makes it must for students. A single cup of pumpkin contains over 200 percent of the

recommended daily intake of vitamin A, making it an outstanding option for optical health.

- The antioxidants in pumpkin could help prevent degenerative damage to the eyes.
- Pumpkin seed oil even helps fight various bacterial and fungal infections. Plus, pumpkin is packed with nearly 20 percent of the recommended amount of daily vitamin C, which may help you recover from colds faster.
- Research has suggested a positive relationship between a diet rich in beta-carotene and a reduced risk of prostate cancer.

Now we know how much pumpkin is important to our health. Below are 10 smart ways to Incorporate Pumpkin into Your Diet:

10 Smart Ways to Incorporate Pumpkin into Your Diet:

1. Pumpkin Oats Cake

When you can't get your mind off dessert, go for our pumpkin and oats cake to the rescue! Spiced with nutmeg and honey, 2-3 slices of this cake are enough to provide required vitamin A for the entire day.

2. Pumpkin Halwa

Give gajar ka halwa a rest for some time and try this exotic Pumpkin halwa. Top it off with roasted coconut flakes, crunchy almonds and go straight to foodie heaven.

3. Roasted Pumpkin

A winner for everyone at the dinner table – bake pumpkin pieces and spice it up with piri-piri masala.

4. Pumpkin Coconut Cookie

Give your regular coconut cookies a twist, add some grated pumpkin along with coconut, and enjoy your healthier cookie.

5. Pumpkin Masala Thepla

This one is my favorite. Add some grated pumpkin in your regular masala thepla and enjoy this breakfast dish.

6.   Whole-Grain   Pumpkin Pancakes

Perfect for winter, this hearty breakfast recipe includes whole-wheat flour, lots of spices, pumpkin, and milk.

7. Pumpkin Tikki

Grate some pumpkin along with your other grated veggies, add some potatoes, roll it in breadcrumbs, shallow fry them and enjoy with tomato sauce.

8. Pasta in Pumpkin Sauce

Creamy pasta dishes are often full of fat and cholesterol. Instead of making your dinner a giant calorie bomb, try pumpkin cream sauce and Greek yogurt instead of heavy cream and make your pasta tastier and healthier.

9. Pumpkin Almond Muffins

Start your day with pumpkin almond muffins. These mouth-watering muffins make for a perfect snack on-the-go and will keep you going until it's time for lunch.

10. Pumpkin Waffles

Combine the flour, sugar, baking soda baking powder, and salt in a medium bowl and stir well. Add the wet ingredients: pumpkin, buttermilk, butter, and vanilla and mix until smooth. Preheat waffle iron. Brush the waffle iron with a little melted butter and cook waffles. Eat with toppings of your choice.

My Thoughts

If you don't like pumpkins just like me but still want to eat it because of its health benefits, then these were my ideas of smartly incorporating pumpkin in the diet which will be tasty yet healthy. And if you are already a Pumpkin lover, then you got some more interesting recipes in your list.

7. PREVENTION IS ACTUALLY BETTER THAN CURE

Prevention is actually better than cure

We all know *Prevention is better than cure* but how many of us apply it in our life? The percentage is very low. Generally, when we see someone having a consequence of their bad habits, we assume that it can only happen to others. We have this tendency where we think bad consequence only happens to others; somewhere we think we are different; this will definitely not going to happen to me. But the fact is, no matter how much you behave irresponsibly toward your health today; it is coming back to you sooner or later, there is no escape.

Sorry if I sounded harsh, but this is the fact. The simple rule is, what you will give to your body, your body will give you back the same. So, if you are giving junk, health deteriorating elements to your body, don't expect it to give you a healthy life in return. Sometimes our body doesn't alarm instantly to junk and bad habits, and everything seems so normal, but with time, it aggregates and then it gives you life-threatening diseases. After all, our body needs good care, good food, good lifestyle and when it doesn't get it, it's function affected, and with time it loses its functionality.

I always hear people talk about their health problems in a way like a god just gave them this problem, not for a second they blame themselves for the problem, they don't even think or analysis what did they do wrong which caused them this particular problem. I believe Prevention is better than cure. You have to analyze what caused you the problem, what was the root of the problem, whether it was the result of your bad eating habit or your bad lifestyle or what exactly went wrong.

We generally, hear that stress cause health problems what if I ask you to think in reverse, what if I tell you that if you will have a health problem then "IT" will give you stress, if you are not feeling healthy in the first place then how will you concentrate on other important aspects of your life? Won't you lose the major opportunities of your life because of your health?

See in this way, if this helps you, God has gifted you this body, you are the caretaker of your body, everything else will come and go, but your body will remain with you for the lifetime.

If you are responsible for anything most, then that's your body. If you will not fulfill your responsibility, then who else will be?

Conclusion

At last, all I can say that your body is not a dustbin where you can throw anything, it is the temple, you should worship it and should think twice before giving it any junk or health deteriorating elements because ultimately what you will give to your body, it will give you back the same.

8. BONUS
COCONUT BURFI SWEET AND
HEALTHY

Coconut Burfi Sweet and Healthy

I like Coconut burfi as it has nuts which are healthy. I am not a sweet tooth, I least prefer sweets, but I made this on a special occasion.

I always substitute an unhealthy ingredient with healthy alternatives in any recipe. So, in Coconut burfi, I have replaced refined white sugar with Brown sugar, if you substitute it with Jaggery, then it will be more beneficial for health. Also, I have substituted normal unsalted butter with cow milk unsalted clarified butter, which is simply **ghee** but made exclusively from cow's milk cream at home. I think if you are a health-conscious but also a sweet tooth, then coconut burfi is the best option you can go for without even second thought.

Health Benefits of Coconut Burfi:

Desiccated coconut:

We all know coconut contains fat but healthy fat, which is very essential for body function. It lowers the levels of LDL (bad cholesterol) and increases the level of good cholesterol or HDL, hence strengthen your arteries, and promote cardiovascular health. Other than that it is very good for skin, it helps in better functioning of the brain. It contains a number of essential nutrients, including dietary fiber, manganese, copper, and selenium.

Cow Ghee (Unsalted clarified butter):

As per Ayurved, cow Ghee is very very good for health. Cow ghee is full of essential nutrients, fatty acids, antibacterial, antifungal, antioxidants, and antiviral properties. It normalizes Vata and Pitta and nourishes the body. It is known as a brain tonic. Excellent for improving memory power and intelligence. Best for strengthening mental health. It is beneficial for curing thyroid dysfunction. It is used to heal wounds, chapped lips, and mouth ulcers. It cures insomnia. Best for lubrication of joints. But it should consume in moderation if you don't want to put on weight.

Jaggery:

Jaggery boosts immunity. One of the most well-known benefits of jaggery is its ability to purify the blood. Jaggery is one of the best natural cleansing agents for the body. It prevents anemia. Controls blood pressure and prevents respiratory problems. Jaggery has a complex carbohydrate that gives energy to the body gradually and for a longer time, therefore, helps in preventing fatigue and weakness of the body.

How I Made Coconut Burfi

Dry Roast Desiccated coconut

Heat 1 tablespoon Cow Ghee (Unsalted clarified butter)

Add cow milk

Bring it to boil and reduce to half

Add brown sugar or jaggery

Add roasted desiccated coconut

and mix well

Add saffron soaked in milk

Pour it in a baking dish

Sprinkle shredded almonds and cut them in squares

Refrigerate for 2 hours and voila Coconut Burfi is ready to eat.

This is how I made Coconut Burfi, and the best part is, you can consume it without worrying about your health. Do try yourself to satisfy your sweet craving.

BOOK 2

Eat So What!
The Power of Vegetarianism

1. WHAT ARE NUTRIENTS? WHY ARE THEY SO IMPORTANT?

What Are Nutrients? Why Are They So Important?

Nutrients are this, nutrients are that, falla food is more nutritious, falla food should not be eaten as it is not nutritious blah blah blah… you may have heard these things thousands of times, so many fusses about nutrition value but the question is what factors decide which food is more nutritious and which one is not? What makes food nutritious? The Answer is the number of nutrients present in a food decides it's nutrition value. Now, what are Nutrients?

This chapter will answer all of your questions about nutrients.

What are Nutrients?

Nutrients are substances present in our food that is essential for our life, providing us energy, essential for repair and growth, regulate chemical processes and necessary for the maintenance of overall health.

I have summarised all about nutrients in the figure below. We will understand each one in detail one by one in this chapter.

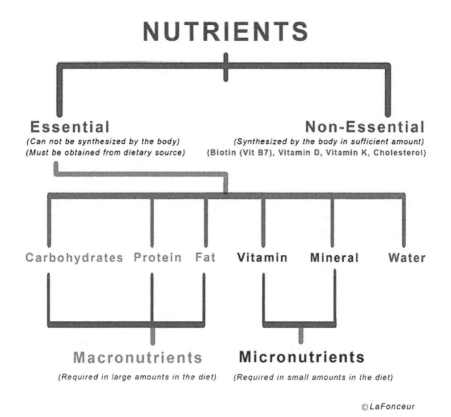

©LaFonceur

Types of Nutrients:

Essential nutrients

Essential nutrients either cannot be synthesized by the body or synthesized in insufficient quantity and are required for normal body functioning thus must be obtained from foods.

Essential nutrients are divided into 2 parts:

Macronutrients

Micronutrients

Macronutrients are the main nutrients that make up the foods that we eat. Body requires these nutrients in relatively large amounts to grow, develop, repair and reproduce. They supply us with energy.

Carbohydrate, protein, and fat are the three macronutrients with fourth bonus water. All these three macronutrients all have their own specific functions in the body. Almost every food has all of the macronutrients but foods are classified based on the highest percentage of macronutrient present in it. For example, a coconut consists up of 50% fat, 10% carbohydrates and 6% protein so this would be classified as a fat, while a banana consists of 80% carbohydrates, with only small amounts of protein and fats so this would be classified as carbohydrate.

1. Carbohydrates

By definition, Carbohydrates, cannot be listed as essential macronutrients as body can synthesize all the carbohydrates on its own but it is recommended to get most of the energy from carbohydrates therefore it is required in relatively large amounts for normal body functioning and is a healthy nutrient choice.

Carbohydrates are comprised of small chains of sugar which the enzyme salivary amylase present in our mouth breaks down into glucose to use as the body's primary energy source and therefore need to make up around 50-65% of a diet. Carbohydrates are important in supplying energy to the brain, improve digestion, play key roles in development, immune system, preventing pathogenesis, and blood clotting

2. Proteins

Proteins are essential macronutrients, consisting of one or more long chain of amino acid which is the essential part of all living organisms, especially as the building blocks of body tissue such as muscle, hair, bones, nails, etc. Among 20 amino acids, nine essential amino acids are essential which cannot be synthesized by the body.

Essential Proteins:

- Histidine
- Isoleucine

- Leucine
- Lysine
- Methionine
- Phenylalanine
- Threonine
- Tryptophan
- Valine

3. Fat

Fat is an essential nutrient that boosts absorption of fat soluble vitamins such as Vitamin A, D, E, K and helps protect internal organs.

Essential Fatty acids:

- Alpha-linolenic acid (omega-3 fatty acid)
- Linoleic acid (omega-6 fatty acid)

Micronutrients are required in small quantities but are as vital as macronutrients for normal body functioning. Micronutrients support metabolism and enable the body to produce hormones, enzymes, and other substances essential for proper growth and development.

Vitamins are organic compounds. They usually act as coenzymes or cofactors for various proteins which are part of many chemical reactions in the body. Vitamin A is vital for healthy skin, teeth, mucus membranes and eye, Vitamin C for immunity, Vitamin D to absorb calcium and promote bone growth and cardiovascular health and Vitamin B6 helps form red blood cells and maintain brain function so they are must have.

Humans require thirteen vitamins in their diet. Vitamins are classified as either water-soluble (vitamin B Complex and vitamin C) or fat-soluble (A, D, E, and K). Water-soluble vitamins dissolve in water and, are readily excreted from the body. This is why the consistent intake of water-soluble vitamins are required. Fat-soluble vitamins require lipid in the body to be absorbed through the intestinal tract.

Essential Vitamins:

Fat soluble vitamins:

- Vitamin A
- Vitamin D

- Vitamin E
- Vitamin K

Water soluble vitamins:

- Vitamin B Complex
  - Thiamine (Vitamin B1)
  - Riboflavin (Vitamin B2)
  - Niacin (Vitamin B3)
  - Pantothenic acid (Vitamin B5)
  - Pyroxidine (Vitamin B6)
  - Biotin (Vitamin B7)
  - Folate (Vitamin B9)
  - Cobalamin (Vitamin B12)
- Vitamin C

Vitamin B7, Vitamin D, and Vitamin H can be synthesized by the body but in insufficient quantity.

Minerals are inorganic and retain their chemical structure. Minerals are mainly needed for metabolism, they are important for healthy bones, needed for muscle contraction, proper fluid balance, and nerve transmission in the body.

Essential Minerals:

Major Minerals

- Calcium
- Sodium
- Potassium
- Magnesium
- Phosphorus

Trace Minerals

- Iodine
- Iron
- Zinc
- Copper
- Chlorine
- Sulfur
- Manganese
- Cobalt
- Molybdenum
- Selenium

Nonessential nutrients

Nonessential nutrients can be synthesized by the body in sufficient quantity or obtained from sources other than foods.

Some examples of Nonessential nutrients:

- Biotin or Vitamin B7 that is produced by gastrointestinal bacteria.

- Vitamin K is produced by intestinal bacteria present in colon.

- Vitamin D is produced by body when skin is exposed to sunlight.

- Cholesterol is produced by the liver in good amount, this is the reason you don't need to add extra cholesterol in your diet.

2. TOP 10 HEALTH BENEFITS OF BEING VEGETARIAN

Top 10 Health Benefits of Being Vegetarian

What is vegetarianism?

Vegetarianism is the practice of abstaining from the consumption of animal products including red meat, fish or other seafood, poultry, the flesh of animal or by-products of animal slaughter. A vegetarian diet includes grains, fruits, vegetables, pulses, nuts, seeds, and with, or without, the use of dairy products and eggs.

There are different types of vegetarians:

- **Lacto-vegetarians** exclude animal products and eggs but eat dairy products.
- **Lacto-ovo-vegetarians** exclude animal products but eat both dairy products and eggs.
- **Jain vegetarians** exclude animal products, eggs, or anything that grows underground including potatoes, onions, and garlic but eat dairy products.
- **Buddhist vegetarians** exclude animal products and vegetables in the allium family

(which have the characteristic aroma of onion and garlic): onion, garlic, chives, scallions, leeks, or shallots but eat dairy products.

- **Vegans** exclude any products derived from animals – no meat, fish, dairy or eggs.

Below are the top 10 health benefits of being vegetarian:

1. Slows the Aging Process, Increases Lifespan

Vegetarian organic plant-based diet is mainly rich in vitamins and minerals, antioxidants, phytonutrients and fiber which in turn strengthens the immune system and flushes out toxin from the body, prevent chemical build up in the body slows down the aging process.

Additionally, a vegetarian diet can prevent many chronic diseases thus facilitating more healthy years and a longer lifespan.

2. Less Toxicity

Toxins such as pesticides, antibiotics, hormones are all fat-soluble, they concentrate in the fatty flesh of the animals. Non-Vegetarian foods can harbor contaminants such viruses and parasites such as toxoplasmosis parasites, Trichinella spiralis, salmonella, and other worms. Food-borne illnesses, bacteria, and chemical toxins are more common in commercial meat, seafood, and poultry when compared with organic plant-based foods.

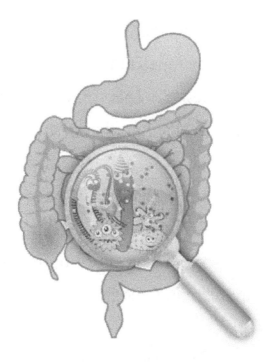

3. Improves Metabolism

Fiber is necessary for proper digestion and fruits and vegetables contain high fiber content. Vegetarian food is easy to digest and helps in fast elimination of toxins and other chemicals from the body keeping the body metabolism in a good state. RMR (resting metabolic rate) in people with a vegetarian diet is higher than omnivores which means vegetarians speedily burn fats.

4. Maintains Healthy Body Weight

Typically, Vegetarians weigh less. Vegetarians tend to have a lower body mass index (a measure of body fat) than meat eaters'. This may be because a vegetarian diet typically comprised of fewer calories and high in fiber-rich such as fruits, and vegetables, grains, legumes, nuts and seeds that are more filling, lower in fat and less calorie dense. This might be the main reason why more and more people today are opting vegetarianism in their life.

5. Reduces Risk of Diabetes

As per a study, diabetes is more frequently occurs in Non-vegetarians almost twice as often as in vegetarians. Vegetarian diet provides greater protection against diabetes. A healthy vegetarian diet is easy to absorb, contains less fatty acids and is nutritious. Vegetarian diets have been shown to be beneficial for people with Type 2 diabetes where weight loss is often the most effective way to manage the condition.

6. Reduces Risk of Cataract

Though it cannot be confirmed that eating meat causes cataract development, but many studies have revealed that decreases in meat consumption as part of a daily diet decreases the risk for cataracts. Researchers suggest that the overall lifestyle of vegetarians contribute to the decreased risk of cataract and vegetarians enjoy less incidence of cataract development.

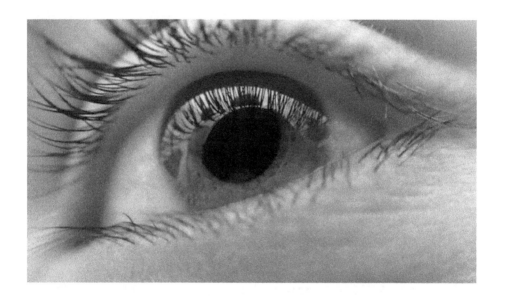

7. Reduces Risk of Cancer

Red meat and processed meat consumption are directly associated with an increase in the risk of colorectal cancer. Regularly consuming is strongly associated with a reduced risk of some cancers.

There is evidence that vegetarians have a statistically significant lower rate of cancer than those who consumed meat regularly. The vegetarian diet contains fruits and vegetables that are high in antioxidants which protect against cancer. Reducing your risk of cancer is another great reason to opt for vegetarianism.

8. Reduces Risk of Heart Disease

Vegetarian diets are rich in fiber, anti-oxidants, and phytonutrients, which are known to reduce oxidative stress and inflammation which may support a significantly reduced the risk of heart disease. Also,

Vegetarian diets are lower in saturated fat and cholesterol in comparison to meat-based diets that are often high in cholesterol, fat and environmental pollutants. Vegetarians have 40 percent less risk of death from cardiovascular disease than non-vegetarians.

9. Gives More Energy

Vegetarians are tending to be more energetic and happy. Meat-based diet is often high in fat and protein making them difficult to digest while vegetarians have a higher consumption of carbohydrates in the form of whole grain.

Carbohydrates digest easily and give energy instantly. Carbohydrates increase serotonin levels, which is mood-boosting neurotransmitter which increases the brain's serotonin levels called happiness hormones which keep you happy all day.

10. Lowers Cholesterol Levels

Vegetarian diet is much low in cholesterol while animal products are very high in cholesterol. High levels of low-density lipoprotein (LDL) cholesterol (bad cholesterol) have been linked with an increased risk of coronary heart disease (CHD).

Vegetarian Diet Is Associated with lower cholesterol levels. This may be due to the Vegetarians have reduced intake of saturated fat, and an increased intake of organic plant-based foods, like fruits, vegetables, whole grains, legumes, seeds, and nuts, which are naturally rich in soluble fiber, soy protein, and plant sterols. Although cholesterol is an essential component of each human cell, there is no need to take cholesterol from an external source as the body can make all the cholesterol it needs from Vegetarian foods.

Conclusion

Along with healthy organic vegetarian diet, there are many factors that attribute to a healthy and long lifespan, some other lifestyles need to pay attention like quitting smoking and drinking. Being on a vegetarian diet doesn't mean you opt for less healthy food options, such as refined grains, which could increase the risk of heart disease. One should follow plant-based diets that are high in fiber, whole grains, vegetables, legumes, seeds and nuts that are lower in fat, more filling, healthy and nutritious.

3. 10 REASONS YOU SHOULD EAT MORE PROTEIN EVERY DAY

10 Reasons You Should Eat More Protein Every Day

What is Protein?

Proteins are essential macronutrients, consisting of one or more long chain of amino acid which is the essential part of all living organisms, especially as the building blocks of body tissue such as muscle, hair, bones, nails, etc.

Daily Recommended Protein Amount

Recommended Dietary Allowances (RDA), the daily dietary intake level of a nutrient considered sufficient to meet your basic nutritional requirements. RDA for protein is 0.8 grams of protein per kilogram of body weight.

RDA is shown below for males and females aged 19-70 years:

Male: 56 g/day

Female: 46 g/day

Below are the 10 reasons you should eat more protein every day:

1. Anti-Aging

Wrinkles are primarily caused by sun damage and loss of the proteins collagen and elastin. As we grow older our body inevitably loses muscle mass. One of the easiest ways to improve your muscle mass and to keep your body healthy is to follow a protein-rich diet which accelerates the healing and nourishing skin. Whey protein is good for anti-aging nutrition it contains branch chain amino acids which heal and nourish skin and prevent aging signs.

2. Speeds Up Recovery from Injury

Protein is an important building block of body tissues, including muscle. Protein can help the body repair after it has been injured. It speeds up the recovery process. Protein digests into the amino acids which are required to repair damaged muscles, the body needs a steady stream of amino acids to promote healing. Protein helps to rebuild any lost muscle. Body needs extra protein post-injury.

The protein-rich diet allows the body to produce new collagen and elastin to help keep tendons and ligaments strong.

3. Boost Muscle Mass

Protein is the building block of muscles. Eating adequate amounts of protein promotes muscle growth and helps in maintaining muscle mass. To gain muscle mass one should do exercise and strength training along with high rich protein diet. Also, the constant supply of Protein throughout the day is essential for optimum muscle growth.

4. Healthy Skin

Protein is a building block of skin tissue. It is great for the general health of skin and for its ability to repair itself. Proteins are broken down into amino acids, for the body's constant reconstruction job. Amino acids help to construct collagen, create lubricating ceramide in the skin which keeps the skin healthy. It also repairs the skin-damaging done by the sun and environmental irritants.

5. Reduces Appetite, Increases Satiety

Protein helps you stay full for longer with less food. Eating a high-protein diet can boost the release of a hunger-suppressing hormone peptide. That means you don't get cravings, and it means you control your hunger. Protein also reduces levels of appetite-spiking hormone ghrelin so you don't get massive cravings at nights. It can make you eat fewer calories automatically.

6. Burns More Calories

When you replace some of carbs and fat with protein in your diet you actually burn more calories as protein gives a boost to your metabolism. This is because our body needs some calories for the purpose of digesting and metabolizing the food. The number of calories required to burn protein into fuel is much higher than fats and carbs, it means your body will burn way more calories over the course of the day. This way your metabolism will be more efficient and you lose more weight.

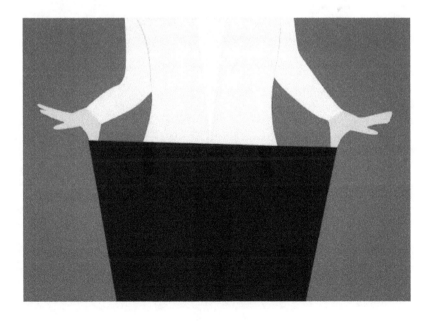

7. Controls Diabetes

A Diet high in protein and low in carbohydrates may help Type 2 diabetes patients improve their blood sugar levels. Protein is broken down into glucose less efficiently than carbohydrate and, as a result, takes longer to reach the bloodstream, cause insulin to release gradually, helping the body maintain healthy glucose levels.

8. Lowers Blood Pressure

Short-term clinical trials suggest that dietary protein lowers blood pressure. High-protein diets might reduce the risk of cardiovascular disease by lowering blood pressure. Increasing protein intake may actually help lower systolic blood pressure. Higher protein diets also characterized by higher fiber intakes lead to a 59% reduction in High Blood Pressure risk.

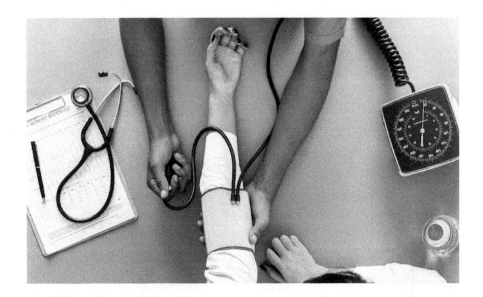

9. Healthy Bones

Osteoporosis is a huge issue especially for women after menopause. Improving bone health is an important component of treating and preventing osteoporosis. Protein represents key nutrients for bone health. Protein is crucial for the body's ability to absorb calcium and grow bones strong. People who eat more protein tend to have a lower risk of osteoporosis and fractures and maintain better bone mass as they age.

10. Healthy Hair

Eating enough protein is important for healthy and strong hair. Protein promotes hair growth because hair follicles are made of mostly protein. Protein-rich diet helps the body to produce keratin, which is fundamental to the hair structure. When keratin weakens, hair strands become dry and brittle. One should eat high protein and iron rich diet to prevent hair loss.

Conclusion

Protein is the basic requirement of the body for repairing, making enzymes, hormones, and other body chemicals. Protein intake should definitely be increased for a healthy life but anything in excess is harmful to health. Too much protein can be harmful to people with kidney disease. Just because protein helps in faster weight lose it is never be advised to completely replace carbs and fats with protein in your diet. Excess of protein may cause bloating, gas, stomach cramps and diarrhea when a lot of protein is fermented in the colon, or if you're low in digestive acids and enzymes.

4. 10 HIGH PROTEIN SOURCES FOR VEGETARIANS

10 High Protein Sources for Vegetarians

Protein is the building blocks of body tissue such as muscle, hair, bones, nails. Protein deficiency is a very common concern about vegetarian diets. However, animal protein is associated with many of the degenerative diseases while vegetable protein isn't.

Sufficient protein intake is a must for all human beings despite the age or gender as higher-protein diets boost muscle mass, faster recovery from injury, healthy skin and weight loss.

Below are the 10 high protein sources for vegetarians:

1. Whey of Cottage Cheese

The liquid portion of the cottage cheese making process is called whey. Whey is a great source of protein for vegetarians. Whey protein can help increase fat loss while providing protein and amino acids, which serve as building blocks for increased muscle growth. You can easily make cottage cheese at home by adding 2 tablespoon lemon juice to 200 ml boiling milk. The acidity of lemon juice will coagulate the milk. Separate the solid and liquid portion. The solid part is the cottage cheese and the remaining liquid is your whey.

2. Peanuts

Peanuts have more protein than any other nuts. In addition, they are loaded with healthful nutrients, such as antioxidants, fiber, iron, and magnesium. Fats in peanuts are healthful fats, which can help lower bad LDL cholesterol and may improve heart health.

100 grams of peanuts contain 26 grams of protein.

Peanuts recipes: Sabudana Khichdi, Crunchy Peanut Chocolate Bars, Roasted Spicy Peanuts.

3. Kidney Beans

Kidney beans are low in fats, are excellent sources of protein. They are also a good source of fiber, vitamins, and minerals. Kidney beans contain all nine-amino acid. They are a good source of lysine, an amino acid which is usually lack in other plant-based protein sources, such as grains.

100 grams of kidney beans contain 24 grams of protein.

Kidney Beans recipes: Mexican Bean Soup, Rajma (Kidney Bean Curry), Vegetarian chili tacos.

4. Oats

Oats contain more protein than most grains. Oat protein is nearly equivalent in quality to soy protein, which is equal to meat, milk and egg protein as per WHO. Oats are one of the easy ways to add protein to your diet.

100 grams of the hull-less oat kernels contain 12-24 grams of protein, the highest among cereals.

Oats recipes: Vegetable Oats Cutlets, Oatmeal Cookies, Oats Upma.

5. Almonds

Almonds are an excellent source of protein. These are also rich in fiber and vitamin E, which is great for the skin. One should eat at least 10 almonds every day, not only for protein but for its other health benefits too. It is advised to eat overnight soaked almonds because it reduces the number of tannins and acids present in the skin of the almond, which can inhibit nutrient uptake by the body.

100 grams of almonds contain 21 grams of protein.

Almonds recipes: Almond Cake, Dry Fruits Milk Shake, Almond Cookies.

6. Chickpeas

Chickpeas are a great source of plant-based protein. There are plenty of chickpeas recipes available which can satisfy your taste bud as well as fulfill your daily protein requirement.

100 grams of chickpeas contain 19 grams of protein.

Chickpeas recipes: Hummus spread, Falafel, Indian Chana masala.

7. Amaranth

Amaranth is a protein powerhouse. Amaranth is high in protein and lysine, an amino acid found in low quantities in other grains. Amaranth grain is free of gluten, which makes it a viable grain for people with gluten intolerance. Amaranth is rich in fiber and also a good source of manganese, magnesium, vitamin B6, phosphorus and iron.

100 grams of amaranth contains 14 grams of protein.

Amaranth recipes: Amaranth and Almond Ladoo, Amaranth cutlets, Amaranth Flour, and Raisin Cookies.

8. Greek Yogurt

Greek yogurt is higher in protein than regular yogurt. Greek yogurt is strained three times, so most of the whey is removed. It also has less carbohydrate than regular yogurt, since some of the whey is removed. Because Greek yogurt is more concentrated, it has more protein than regular yogurt.

100 grams of Greek yogurt contains 10 grams of protein.

Greek Yogurt recipes: Greek Yogurt Pancakes, Salad with Greek Yogurt Dressing, Pasta in Greek Yogurt Sauce.

9. Tofu

Tofu, also known as bean curd. Just like cottage cheese, tofu is prepared by coagulating soy milk and then pressing the resulting curds into solid white blocks. Tofu is the richest source of protein as it contains all nine essential amino acids. It is also a valuable source of iron, calcium, copper, zinc, vitamin B1, phosphorous, manganese, and selenium.

100 grams of tofu contains 8 grams of protein.

Tofu recipes: Tofu Nuggets, Asian Garlic Tofu, Tofu Manchurian.

10. Green Peas

Peas are a complete protein, containing all nine essential amino acids. Along with protein, peas have a high level of Vitamin K. In addition, peas are a good source of dietary fiber, Vitamin A, Vitamin C, iron, folate, thiamin, and manganese.

Both fresh and dried green peas are higher in protein. You can soak the dried green peas in plenty of water, overnight, or for 6-8 hours. Drain the soaking water. Place this in a pressure cooker with 2 cups of fresh water. Pressure cook for 1 whistle. Now it is ready to use in your recipes.

100 grams of Peas contain 6 grams of protein.

Green Peas recipes: Green Peas Cutlet, Peas Fried Rice, Peas and Mint Soup.

My Thoughts

Protein is an important building block of bones, muscles, nails. Our body requires protein for repairing and making enzymes, hormones, and other chemicals of the body. Insufficient protein intake in vegetarians is not uncommon. The above listed protein-rich foods are readily available in the market and one can easily include them in their diet.

5. 10 REASONS WHY FAT IS NOT THE ENEMY. THE TRUTH ABOUT FATS!

10 Reasons Why Fat is Not the Enemy. The Truth About Fats!

Did you know that the human brain is made up of nearly 60% fat? Fat is not something we should run from; our bodies need a certain amount of fat to work at their best. Not all fats are bad, not all Fats are good. Let's just quickly see which type of fat is our friend and which one is our enemy.

Type of fats:

Trans fats

Trans fat is the *worst* type of dietary fat. The hydrogenation process is used to turn healthy oils into solids to prevent them from becoming rancid and a byproduct of this process is Trans fats. Trans fats have no known health benefits and that there is no safe level of consumption. It is better to check the Nutritional Facts given on the packet of your packed food for any presence of Trans fat. For every 2% of calories from trans fat consumed daily, the risk of heart disease rises by 23%.

Food containing Trans Fat:

- Solid margarine

- French fries
- Vegetable shortening
- Pastries
- Cookies

Saturated Fats

They are solid at room temperature. A diet rich in saturated fats can drive up total cholesterol, and tip the balance toward more harmful LDL cholesterol, which prompts blockages to form in arteries in the heart and elsewhere in the body. Saturated fats should consume in moderation and nutrition experts recommend limiting saturated fat to fewer than 10% of calories a day.

Common sources of saturated fat:
- Whole milk
- Cheese
- Red meat
- Coconut oil
- Many commercially prepared baked goods

Monounsaturated and Polyunsaturated Fats

Monounsaturated and Polyunsaturated fats are healthy fats. Healthy fats are liquid at room temperature, not solid. These fats come mainly from vegetables, nuts, seeds, and fish. Polyunsaturated fats are used to build cell membranes and the covering of nerves. They are needed for blood clotting, muscle movement, and inflammation.

There are two broad categories of healthy fats: Monounsaturated

Polyunsaturated fats

Good sources of monounsaturated fats are

- Extra virgin olive oil
- Sunflower oils
- Peanut oil
- Canola oil
- High-oleic safflower oil
- Avocados
- Nuts

Polyunsaturated fats include omega-3 fatty acids and omega-6 fatty acids. Eating polyunsaturated fats in place of saturated fats or highly refined carbohydrates reduces harmful LDL cholesterol and improves the cholesterol profile. It also lowers triglycerides.

Good sources of omega-6 fatty acids include

- Corn oil
- Sunflower oil
- Safflower oil
- Soybean oil
- Walnut

Omega-6 fatty acids have also been linked to protection against heart disease.

Good sources of omega-6 fatty acids include

- Corn oil
- Sunflower oil
- Safflower oil
- Soybean oil
- Walnut

Below are the 10 reasons why fat is not the enemy:

1. Fat is Essential to Brain Health

Fat is essential to brain health. The brain is made of 60% fats, out of which a large chunk is docosahexaenoic acid (DHA) or Omega 3 fats.

Essential vitamins such as A, D, E and K are not water soluble and require fat to get transported and absorbed by the body. These vitamins are crucial for brain health and many of our vital organs.

Vitamin D decreases susceptibility to Alzheimer's, Parkinson's, depression and other brain disorders and omega 3 is said to sharpen the cognitive function as well as to improve mood.

2. Fat for Better Skin

Fat makes up the bulk of the cellular membrane and our skin is made up of a very large number of cells. Without the proper consumption of fat, our skin can become dry and chapped, which can also open up pathways for infection to enter our bodies.

3. Fat Boosts Immune System

We need fats for a healthy immune system. Saturated fats play an important role here as adequate amounts will help the immune system recognize and then destroy foreign invaders.

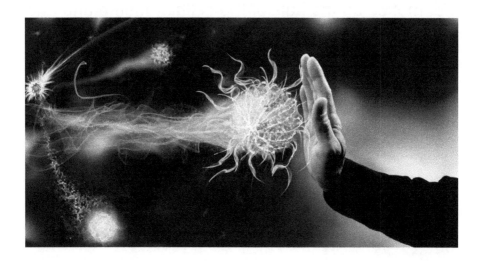

4. Fat Keeps Our Lungs Working Properly

A thin layer that coats the lungs is 100% saturated fatty acids? We need fats in to protect this protective layer, or we could suffer from breathing difficulties.

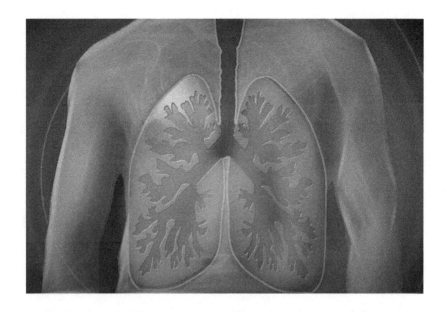

5. Fat is Good for Heart

Unsaturated fats are good for the heart because they

help lower blood pressure and reduce triglycerides, a type of fat in your blood, which slows the build-up of plaque in arteries. Switching from saturated fats to polyunsaturated or monounsaturated fats can lower the risk of heart disease by up to 25%.

6. Fat Can Help You Lose Weight *(Yes, you read it right)*

Hungry cells cause weight gain. When we restrict our calories, our bodies go into a starvation mode holding onto calories and storing fat.

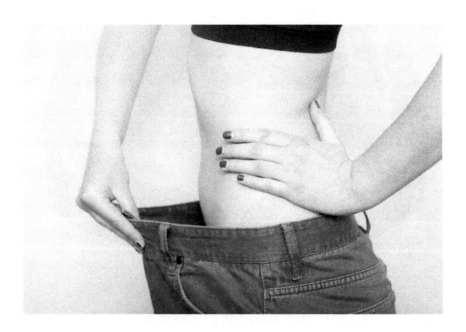

When we fuel our bodies with the right foods, and enough healthy fats your metabolism keeps running and you are better able to lose weight.

7. Fat for Proper Insulin release

Saturated fats found in things like coconut oil and butter help support proper nerve signaling by acting on signaling messengers. These messengers directly affect metabolism, as well as control the proper release of insulin.

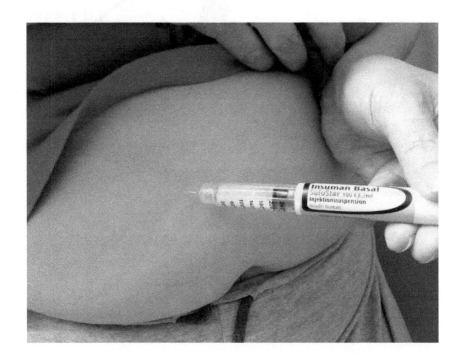

8. Fat for Stronger Bones and Less Risk of Osteoporosis

The important bone-building vitamins – Vitamin A, D, E and K are only fat soluble, which means they are transported and absorbed using dietary fats. Fats are needed for the metabolism of calcium.

9. Fat for Better Reproductive Health

Fats are the building blocks for healthy cell membranes, but they are also important for hormonal health. Sex hormones – testosterone, estrogen, progesterone – are all made of cholesterol. Cutting way back on dietary fats can increase your risk of hormonal problems like hypothyroidism, menstrual irregularities, and low testosterone levels for men.

10. Fat for Better Eye Health

Omega-3 fats may benefit individuals with dry eye disease by helping them produce more tears. With this condition, a lack of tears causes dryness, discomfort and occasional blurry vision. omega-3 fats have anti-inflammatory properties which may play a role in the prevention of diabetic retinopathy.

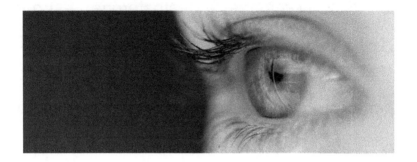

Conclusion

No doubt all fats are not good for health but at the same time, certain types of fats are essential for our health. Try to consume monounsaturated and polyunsaturated fats as much as you can (not beyond the limit) and limit your saturated fats consumption less than 10%. Try to substitute butter to extra virgin olive oil, French fries to nuts. These small changes in diet will result in a healthier and longer life.

6. TOP 10 HEALTHY FAT FOODS YOU SHOULD EAT

Top 10 Healthy Fat Foods You Should Eat

From decades fat is associated with weight gain, heart diseases and many more. But now is the time you understand all types of fats are not the devil. If you are avoiding fats but have no control over sugar, processed and refined carbs consumption then it is more dangerous to your health. Fat not only stores energy but insulate us and protect our vital organs. In fact, healthy fats boost your heart health, improve cholesterol level and enhance your beauty by making your skin glowing and hair shiny.

Now the question arises, what are the healthy fats? How would you differentiate between good fats and bad fats? The answer is simple, focus more on foods rich in Unsaturated fats - Monounsaturated and Polyunsaturated but don't 100% avoid Saturated fat.

Below I have listed top 10 healthy fat source which you should eat for health and nutrition benefits.

1. Ghee

Ghee is a form of clarified butter. It is generally used in Indian cooking. Ghee made from cow milk has immense health benefits as per Ayurved. Cow ghee is full of essential nutrients, fatty acids, antioxidants. It has antibacterial, antifungal, and antiviral properties. Ghee is rich in conjugated linoleic acid, or CLA, a fatty acid known to be protective against carcinogens, diabetes, and artery plaque. It is known as a brain tonic and excellent for improving memory power and intelligence. It is beneficial for curing thyroid dysfunction. It is used to heal wounds, chapped lips, and mouth ulcers. It also cures insomnia and is best for lubrication of joint.

Ghee has a high smoke point which means ghee doesn't go rancid even at high temperature and retain all the important nutrients that provide all the wonderful ghee benefits. Ghee is a rich source of vitamin A, vitamin E and vitamin K, keeping your skin glowing and maintaining healthy vision. Vitamin K found in ghee helps in preventing calcium deposits in the arteries that can obstruct blood flow and lead to blockages. Ghee should consume in moderation if you don't want to put on weight. 1 tablespoon (15g) of ghee in a day is enough to ripe all the health benefits of ghee.

2. Extra Virgin Olive Oil

Extra virgin olive oil is one of the world's healthiest oils. Eating about 2 tablespoons of Extra virgin olive oil daily may reduce the risk of coronary heart disease due to the monounsaturated fat in olive oil. Extra virgin olive oil is loaded with powerful antioxidants which inhibit oxidation and prevent the formation of free radicals in the body which reduce the risk of chronic diseases and cancer.

Extra virgin Olive oil shouldn't be used for cooking at high temperatures such as deep-frying, as it oxidizes quicker than other oils.

3. Coconut & Coconut Oil

Lauric acid is the reason why coconut considers as a healthy fat despite the fact that it contains almost 89% of saturated fat. Lauric acid is a saturated fatty acid with a 12-carbon atom chain that has antibacterial, antiviral, and antimicrobial property. This potentially helps to prevent infections. Coconut oil is good for your skin and hair.

Coconut oil has anti-inflammatory property due to antioxidants present in it which help to potentially reduce arthritis symptoms. Saturated fat in coconut oil increases HDL levels (good cholesterol) and promotes heart health but at the same time it increases LDL (bad cholesterol) too therefore, it should be used in moderation.

4. Avocado

Avocado is loaded with vitamin B complex, vitamin K, vitamin C, and vitamin E. It is also rich in phytosterols and carotenoids such as lutein and zeaxanthin which have the ability to be converted to vitamin A and protect eyes from diseases because they absorb damaging blue light that enters the eyes. Vitamin K in avocado can support bone health by increasing calcium absorption.

Dietary fiber in avocado Improves digestion. About 75% of an avocado's calories come from fat, most of which is monounsaturated fat MUFAs (about 65%) as oleic acid, linoleic acid which are strongly associated with reduced risks of heart disease, high blood pressure, and diabetes.

5. Flaxseed

Flaxseed is high in unsaturated omega-3 fatty acids: alpha-linolenic acid (ALA). which protect against heart disease by improving blood pressure. Only 1-2 tablespoons of Flaxseed are enough to reap the benefits.

Flaxseed contains both soluble and insoluble fiber, which keep you feeling fuller longer, facilitate weight-loss as well as reduce cholesterol level. Regular consumption of flaxseed is good for your skin and heart. Flaxseeds contain other nutrients as well as protein, magnesium, calcium, phosphorous, omega 3 and lignin. Regular consumption of flax seeds is good for your skin. Lignans in flaxseeds have antioxidant and estrogen properties which prevent cancer.

6. Black Sesame Seeds

Black sesame seeds are high in unsaturated fatty acids while low in saturated fatty acids. Black sesame seeds are considered as one of the best anti-aging foods as per traditional Chinese Medicine. Sesame seeds are rich in calcium, magnesium, and copper which are the bone-forming minerals.

The oleic acid and linoleic acid in black sesame seeds promote skin softening and cell regeneration which improves skin health. The higher iron content of black sesame seeds helps in preventing iron deficiency anemia.

7. Walnut

Unlike most nuts walnuts are high in polyunsaturated fatty acids, omega-3 fat particularly alpha-linolenic acid (ALA), linoleic acid and oleic acid which protects against heart disease.

Eat walnuts for better brain function and better memory. Walnuts may help lower blood pressure.

The anti-inflammatory property of walnut reduces the risk of breast and prostate cancers. Antioxidants in walnut are of higher quality and potency than in any other nut.

8. Almond

Almonds have high levels of monounsaturated and polyunsaturated and have a significant positive impact on cholesterol levels.

Protein and fiber content of almonds make them the best option for a snack because a handful of almonds can satisfy you for at least a few hours, increasing the chance of losing weight successfully. Biotin (also known as vitamin H) in almonds improve hair health. Almonds are a great source of vitamin E and anti-oxidants which Improve Skin Health.

9. Dark chocolate

Dark chocolate is a great source of flavanols, a powerful anti-oxidant which has the ability to lower blood pressure and get more blood flowing to the heart, hence improve heart health. Though half of the dark chocolate fat content is saturated, it is also a good source of vitamins A, B, and E, iron, calcium, potassium, magnesium.

Also, Dark chocolate helps improve cognitive performance but be sure eat chocolate with 70 percent cocoa for the highest levels of flavonoids and avoid milk chocolate, which contains loads of sugar and dairy.

10. Dairy

Cow's Milk is good for the bones because it offers a rich source of calcium, a mineral essential for healthy bones and teeth. Cow's milk is a source of potassium, which can reduce blood pressure, and risk of cardiovascular disease.

Some available **Cheese** options are healthy as they fulfill the body's calcium and potassium need. cottage cheese, Feta, ricotta are the top healthiest cheese options available.

Probiotic yogurt helps keep the intestines healthy and strengthen the digestive tract. Probiotic yogurt increases the good bacteria in your gut to promote better overall health. Daily intake of probiotic yogurt, boosts immunity and reduces cholesterol levels.

Conclusion

Fats are an important dietary requirement. Healthy fats not only provide energy but also protect our vital organs by insulating body organs against shock. Fat-soluble vitamins such as vitamins A, D, E, and K can only be digested and absorbed in conjunction with fats. This proves fats are not the enemy. Start adding healthy fats in your diet from today. Happy eating.

7. 10 REASONS YOU SHOULD NEVER GIVE UP CARBOHYDRATES

10 Reasons You Should Never Give Up Carbohydrates

The main function of carbohydrates is to provide the body and brain with energy. Just like your car needs fuel to make it run, your body needs carbohydrates to make it go.

What are carbs?

Carbohydrates are one of three macronutrients — along with proteins and fats — that your body requires daily. There are three main types of carbohydrates: starches, fiber, and sugars.

Starches are often referred to as complex carbohydrates. They are found in grains, legumes, and starchy vegetables, like potatoes and corn (*Preferable carbs*).

Sugars are known as simple carbohydrates. There are natural sugars in vegetables, fruits, milk, and honey. Added sugars are found in processed foods, syrups, sugary drinks and sweets (*Avoidable Carbs*).

After you enjoy a meal, the carbohydrates from the foods you consumed are broken down into smaller units of sugar. These small units get absorbed out of your digestive tract and into your bloodstream. This blood sugar, or blood glucose, is transported through your bloodstream to supply energy to your muscles and other tissues. This is an important process; in fact, of the different functions of carbohydrates, **supplying energy to the body is the main role**.

You should be getting at least 200 to 400 grams of carbs every day. Still not convinced carbs are fine? Then pay attention to these 10 important benefits of eating carbs:

10 reasons you should never give up carbohydrates:

1. Want to Increase Your IQ Level, Have Carbohydrates

Most of your body cells use the simple carbohydrate glucose for energy, but your brain is particularly in need of glucose as an energy source. So, we can add that an important function of carbs is supplying energy to the brain. If you have ever gone on a low-carb diet and felt like your brain was foggy for a few days, then you experienced just how important carbohydrates are to proper brain function.

2. Carbs Can Help Boost Your Mood

Researchers suspect that carbs promote the production of serotonin, a feel-good brain chemical. In a study from the Archives of Internal Medicine, people who followed a very low carbohydrate diet for a year—which allowed only 20 to 40 grams of carbs daily, about the amount in just 1/2 cup of rice plus one piece of bread—experienced more depression, anxiety, and anger than those assigned to a low-fat, high-carb diet that focused on low-fat dairy, whole grains, fruit, and beans.

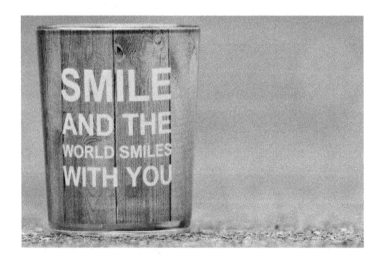

3. Carbs Can Help Prevent Weight Gain—and Even Promote Weight Loss

Researchers at Brigham Young University in Utah followed the eating habits of middle-aged women for nearly two years and found that those who increased their fiber intake generally lost weight. Women who decreased the fiber in their diets gained. Many carbohydrates contain dietary fiber, which is actually an indigestible complex carbohydrate.

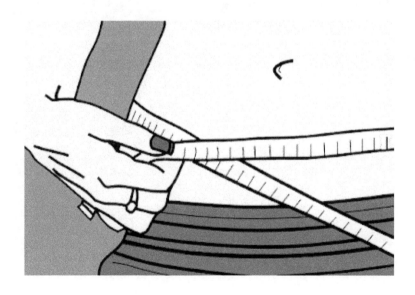

4. Good for Your Heart

Research suggests that increasing your soluble-fiber intake (a type of fiber found in carb-rich foods like oatmeal and beans) by 5 to 10 grams each day could result in a 5 percent drop in "bad" LDL cholesterol. Similarly, people who eat more whole grains (think brown rice, bulgur, and quinoa) also tend to have lower LDL cholesterol and higher "good" HDL cholesterol.

5. Improved Sleep Pattern

Foods rich in slow digesting carbohydrates also contribute to restful sleep, thanks once more to serotonin. In addition to improving your mood, the neurotransmitter serotonin also helps ensure you experience restful sleep. Diets that are low in carbohydrates have a harder time synthesizing serotonin, with insomnia a probable outcome. This is why milk is considered an effective nightcap, even though it is not the best carbohydrate option.

6. Reduced Cancer Risk

This is a catch-22 and depends a lot on which carbohydrates you opt for. While most people will think of things like potatoes when considering food options, there are in reality tons more of options that may have never crossed your mind. For example, onions, tomatoes, bell peppers and hundreds of vegetables can all be considered carbohydrates at their core, even though what they bring to the table are vastly different. And these are the carbohydrates you should be aiming for. These are loaded with anti-oxidants, and help to combat abnormal cellular growth.

The high fiber nature of these foods also helps to promote waste and cholesterol removal. These wholesome carbohydrate foods also fight early-stage cancer, as the cells require glucose as their primary source of fuel. Consuming foods that very slowly convert to glucose can reduce the supply of nutrients to them, and cell death or apoptosis may occur.

7. Improved Digestion

Getting enough fiber-rich carbohydrates can help prevent digestive problems, such as constipation and indigestion. Insoluble fiber, the type of fiber that doesn't break down during digestion, is also known as roughage. It pushes other food along your digestive tract, speeding up the digestive process. It also adds bulk to your stool, making it easier to pass bowel movements. Without sufficient intake of carbohydrates, you may not get enough fiber to keep your digestive system regular.

8. Improve Blood Pressure

High blood pressure is one of the strongest known risk factors for stroke and heart disease. Lowering blood pressure is therefore considered a very important step to lower the risk of cardiovascular disease. Studies indicate that diet rich in carbohydrates lower blood pressure in individuals with overweight or obesity.

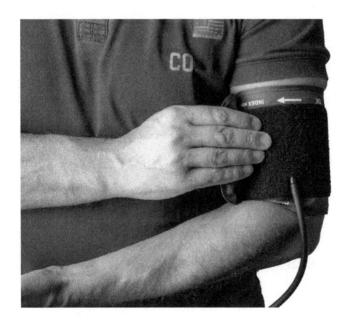

9. Increase Energy Levels

Carbohydrates are the body's primary energy source, as it is eventually converted in glucose which is necessary for the production of ATP- the energy currency used in our body. Diets low in carbohydrates need to take intermediate steps to facilitate the production of glucose, supplementing it with other alternative energy sources. If you are feeling lethargic, a meal with quality carbohydrates is usually sufficient to get you out the rut.

10. Can Improve Your Lifespan

Carbohydrate-rich foods stimulate the production of two anabolic hormones, insulin and insulin-like growth factor 1 (IGF-1). IGF-1 is involved in cellular recovery and rejuvenation and can help keep your cellular age well beyond what you chronologically are. Carbohydrates also stimulate growth hormone production, another key anti-aging hormone.

My Thoughts

Though there are many benefits of carbohydrates, you need to make sure you're eating them in moderation. Though carbohydrates containing food groups boast a host of vitamins and minerals needed by the body, eating any food group in excess can result in weight gain. Consulting with your physician or a registered dietitian can help you determine the amount of carbohydrate best for your health goals and existing health conditions.

8. 10 HEALTHY CARBOHYDRATES YOU MUST EAT FOR HEALTH AND NUTRITION BENEFITS

10 Healthy Carbohydrates You Must Eat for Health and Nutrition Benefits

What are Carbs/Carbohydrates?

Carbohydrates are one of three macronutrients — along with proteins and fats — that your body requires daily.

Simple carbohydrates are carbohydrates that contain single monosaccharide units. They are broken down quickly by the body to be used as energy. They are found in natural food sources such as milk, milk products, fruit, and vegetables.

Complex carbohydrates are polysaccharides which are made up of complex chains of thousands of monosaccharide units. Complex carbohydrates digest slowly and take time to absorb to the body. They are found in whole grains, legumes, and starchy vegetables, like potatoes.

Why carbs are important?

The main function of carbohydrates is to provide the body and brain with energy. Carbohydrates improve brain power, reduce cancer risk, improve digestion and sleep pattern.

Below is the list of 10 high-quality carbohydrates that you must eat for health and nutrition benefits:

1. Whole Wheat

Unlike unhealthy Refined wheat which is processed to remove the bran and the germ, leaving only the endosperm, whole-wheat is made from the entire wheat kernels—bran, germ, and endosperm which makes them highly nutritious.

Gluten is a group of proteins, occur with starch in the endosperm of wheat, as refined wheat or white flour only consist of endosperm, gluten is quite high in them. Amount of gluten present in 3 cups of whole wheat flour is equivalent to the amount of gluten present in 1 cup of white flour.

Whole wheat is a rich source of vitamin B6, dietary fiber, iron, calcium, potassium, magnesium, etc. Whole wheat has plenty of complex carbohydrates which give sustained energy. Bran from whole wheat provides dietary fiber which helps in reducing blood cholesterol levels and may lower risk of heart disease.

100 g of Whole wheat flour contains 72 g of total carbohydrates, of which 11 g is dietary fiber.

2. Brown Rice

Brown rice is whole-grain rice from which only inedible the husk (the outermost layer) is removed while from white rice, along with the hull, the bran layer and the germ (the next layers underneath the husk) are also removed, leaving mostly the starchy endosperm. Several vitamins and dietary minerals are lost in this removal and the further polishing process.

Brown rice is a good source of vitamin B1, B2, B6,

magnesium, selenium, phosphorus, and is high in fiber. Brown rice is considered a low glycemic index food as it digests more slowly, causing a lower change in blood sugar level. The soluble fiber in brown rice attaches to cholesterol particles and takes them out of the body, helping to reduce overall cholesterol levels and may help prevent the formation of blood clots.

100 g of raw brown rice contains 73 g of total carbohydrate, of which 3.52 g is dietary fiber.

3. Oats

Oat groats are the whole form of oats, these are mostly intact, hulled oat grains. Groats include the cereal germ and fiber-rich bran portion of the grain, as well as the endosperm.

For steel cuts oats, oats groats are processed by chopping the whole oat groat into several pieces. For rolled oats, oats groats are first steamed to make them soft, then pressed to flatten them. For instant oats, oats groats pre-cooked, dried, and then pressed slightly thinner than rolled oats.

Steel cuts oats are slightly higher in fiber than rolled while Instant oats are the most highly processed variety and have quite less nutritional value. Oat groats are the healthiest among all types of oats. You can coarsely grind oat groats into flour and use this flour in making bread, cookies, and chapattis.

Oats are gluten-free whole grain and an excellent source of protein, dietary fiber, antioxidants, vitamins, and minerals, especially manganese.

Oat is a rich source of the water-soluble fiber β-glucan which help keep cholesterol in check, may help manage diabetes. Oats promote healthy bacteria in the digestive tract, help fight cardiovascular disease, and Type 2 diabetes.

100 g of oats contain 66.3 g of total carbohydrate, of which 11g is dietary fiber, 4 g of soluble fiber β-glucan.

4. Quinoa

Quinoa is a seed-producing flowering plant. It is pseudocereal which means unlike wheat and rice, quinoa is not a grass but are used in much the same way as cereals. Quinoa seed can be ground into flour and otherwise used as cereals.

Quinoa is high in complex carbohydrate, insoluble fiber, and protein which makes it very filling. It has complete protein, means it contains all nine essential amino acids. It is also high in iron, magnesium, calcium, potassium, B vitamins, vitamin E, phosphorus, vitamin E and antioxidants.

Another good part is quinoa is gluten-free, so people with gluten intolerance can eat quinoa to meet their daily recommended carbs requirement.

Quinoa has the anti-inflammatory property, regulate body temperature, aids enzyme activity.

100 g of raw quinoa contains 64.2 g of complex carbohydrate, of which 7 g is dietary fiber.

5. Sweet Potatoes

Sweet potatoes are a rich source of fiber as well as containing an array of vitamins and minerals including iron, calcium, selenium, and they're a good source of most of our B vitamins and vitamin C. One of the key nutritional benefits of sweet potatoes are that they're high in an antioxidant known as beta-carotene, which converts to vitamin A once consumed.

Raw sweet potatoes are rich in complex carbohydrates and are a rich source of dietary fiber as well as containing an array of vitamins such as B vitamins and vitamin C, moderately contain vitamin B5, vitamin B6, and minerals including iron, calcium, selenium, manganese. One of the key nutritional benefits of sweet potatoes are that they're high in beta-carotene, an antioxidant which converts to vitamin A once consumed in the body.

Sweet potatoes protect the body from free radicals protects against cancer, Support Immune System, Support Healthy Vision.

100 g of sweet potatoes contain 20 g of complex carbohydrate, of which 3 g is dietary fiber.

6. Boiled Potatoes

Boiled potatoes have a lower glycemic score than naked baked potatoes. Because of the lower glycemic score, our body digest boiled potatoes more slowly make them easier to digest and keep us feeling full longer.

Boiled potatoes cooked with skin are very low in Saturated Fat, Sodium, contain zero cholesterol.

A large, unpeeled boiled potato is rich in B-complex vitamins. A boiled potato provides more than half of the recommended daily intake of vitamin B6. It is also a good source of, Potassium and Copper, and a very good source of Vitamin C.

It contains resistant Starch that improves Gut health by making more good bacteria and less bad bacteria in the gut. Moreover, boiled potatoes are gluten-free.

100 g of boiled potatoes contain 20 g of total carbohydrate, of which 1.6 g is dietary fiber.

7. Apples

For the greatest health benefits, eat the whole apple - both skin and flesh. Apples are extremely rich in dietary fiber. The soluble fiber content of apples may promote weight loss and gut health.

1 medium-sized apple contains 95 calories, it takes 150 calories to digest an apple. It means you will burn an additional 50 calories simply by eating an apple.

Apples are highly rich in important antioxidants, flavonoids. The phytonutrients and antioxidants in apples may help reduce the risk of developing diabetes, hypertension, heart disease, and cancer.

Other health benefits of apples include prevention of stomach, and liver disorders, anemia, gallstones, and constipation.

100 g of apples contain 14 g of total carbohydrate, of which 2.4 g is dietary fiber.

8. Bananas

Bananas are high in potassium, that promotes heart health. Eating them could help lower blood pressure and reduce the risks of cancer and asthma. Bananas are rich in fiber, calcium, vitamin B6, vitamin C, and various antioxidants and phytonutrients. Unripe bananas have a high content of resistant starch which promotes intestinal health.

Bananas have a low glycemic index. Due to the high iron content, bananas are good for those suffering from anemia. Bananas have a decent amount of magnesium, which has been known to aid sound sleep.

100 g of bananas contain 23 g of total carbohydrate, of which 2.6 g is dietary fiber.

9. Chickpeas

Chickpeas are high in complex carbohydrates which make you feel full for a longer period of time as they digest slowly. The starch found in chickpeas is digested slowly and supports more stabilized blood sugar levels. Chickpeas are high in protein which helps in weight loss. The fiber in chickpeas absorb water and attach to toxins and waste as they move through the digestive system, forming stool, which contains toxins and waste that must be removed from the body.

They are a rich source of the essential vitamin B complex (B1, B2, B3 B6, B12), vitamin A, vitamin C, and vitamin K, antioxidants and minerals such as iron, magnesium, zinc, phosphorous and folate.

100 g of chickpeas contain 61 g of total carbohydrate, of which 17 g is dietary fiber.

10. Kidney Beans

Kidney beans contain both soluble and insoluble fiber, which keep your digestive system running smoothly. Soluble fiber can bind cholesterol in the intestine and remove it from the body and insoluble fiber adds bulk to the stool and helps prevent constipation.

They contain slow carbohydrates which means the carbohydrates break down and are absorbed from the intestines slowly avoiding sudden blood sugar spikes. Antioxidants found in kidney beans help combat cancer. Additionally, calcium and magnesium in kidney beans can prevent osteoporosis and strengthen the bones. Kidney beans are among the richest sources of plant-based protein which boost muscle mass.

100 g of kidney beans contain 6 g of total carbohydrate, of which 25 g is dietary fiber.

Conclusion

Health benefits of high-quality carbohydrates rich food are countless. Don't confuse healthy carbs with refined processed carbs such as cookies, donuts. To meet recommended daily carbs need one should never depend upon refined carbs. Add high-quality carbohydrates into your diet for a healthy life.

Carbohydrate-restricted diets possess possible risks of osteoporosis and cancer incidence. But one should keep this in mind that eating carbs in excess may result in weight gain.

Preventive Measures…..

*Vegetarian foods can prevent you from many diseases, it adds valuable and healthy years to your life, however, some essential nutrients are found in lesser quantity in plant-based vegetarian food, having said that there is no essential nutrient which can't be found in vegetarian food. In general, vegetarians diet is 60-70% comprised of carbohydrates and protein intake of vegetarians are less in compare to non- vegetarians which many times lead to protein deficiency. Therefore, being a vegetarian you must eat an adequate amount of protein in your diet daily, you can find the **list of protein-rich foods** in chapter 4 of this book.*

Other health issues which vegetarians face are

Iron Deficiency Anemia

Vitamin B12 Deficiency

Fortunately, prevention from these conditions doesn't cost you physician fees. In fact, prevention from these conditions doesn't require fancy costly foods, you can prevent them by smart eating. All you need to add some simple foods in your diet and you are fit inside out. Let's discuss both conditions one by one in detail.

9. 10 POWER FOODS TO EAT TO GET RID OF ANEMIA

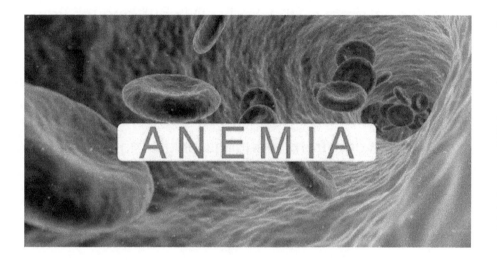

10 Power Foods to Eat to Get Rid of Anemia

What is Anemia?

Iron Deficiency Anemia is a common type of Anemia- a condition in which there is a deficiency of red cells or of hemoglobin in the blood.

As the name implies iron deficiency anemia is due to insufficient iron in the body. Without enough iron, body can't produce enough of hemoglobin in red blood cells. Hemoglobin is the main part of red blood cells and binds oxygen. Hemoglobin in the blood carries oxygen from the lungs or gills to the rest of the body.

Cause of Anemia

Iron deficiency is amongst the most common of nutritional deficiencies and the most common cause of anemia globally, although other conditions, such as folate, vitamin B12 and vitamin A deficiencies, can all cause anemia.

Inadequate iron intake due to poor diet, blood loss through heavy periods, inflammatory bowel disease and increased requirements during pregnancy lead to anemia.

Symptoms of Anemia

Iron deficiency anemia signs and symptoms may include:

- Fatigue
- Dizziness
- Cold hands and feet
- Weakness
- Pale skin
- Irregular heartbeats
- Shortness of breath, particularly with exercise

With proper diet, rich in iron one can get rid of anemia.

Heme Iron and Non-Heme Iron

The two forms of dietary iron are Heme Iron and Non-Heme Iron: Heme iron is the type of iron that comes from animal proteins like seafood, meat, poultry, and fish.

Iron from plants is known as non-heme iron and is found in plant-based foods like grains, fruits, beans, vegetables, fruits, nuts, and seeds and in iron-fortified foods such as oats.

Vitamin C helps your stomach absorb iron. Try to combine non-heme iron foods with vitamin C (for example, a glass of lemon juice, orange, berries, kiwi fruit, tomatoes, and capsicum) to increase absorption of iron.

As this is a vegetarian zone we will discuss vegetarian options in detail.

Below is the list of 10 power foods to eat to get rid of anemia:

1. Spinach

Spinach is rich in Iron, beta-carotene, calcium, vitamin B9 and C and fiber. Regular consumption of spinach can prevent anemia. Spinach is much better than red meat as it provides fewer calories and is fat and cholesterol free. To make the most of its health benefits, include spinach in your daily diet. Make sure to combine vitamin-C-rich foods such as citrus fruits with spinach to improve absorption.

2. Beetroot

Beetroot is loaded with iron and vitamin C, which is considered good for anemia. Beetroot helps in repairing and reactivating the red blood cells in the body. Once activated, oxygen can easily be transferred to the muscles and other tissues of the body. Adding beetroot in any form in your daily diet will help to easily fight anemia.

3. Lentils

Legumes—especially lentils—are great for anemia, as just a half-cup has around 20% of iron what your body needs for the day. Legumes are also high in folate, magnesium, potassium, and fiber that fills you up may help lower cholesterol and may help stabilize your blood sugar and may even aid weight loss.

4. Honey

Honey is among the most popular and widely used sweetener with enormous health benefits. Honey is a rich source of iron. Along with Iron, copper, and magnesium in honey increase hemoglobin concentration in your blood, thereby treating anemia. Adding one tablespoon of honey to a glass of lukewarm water with some lemon juice early in the morning on an empty stomach every day will help in effectively fighting anemia.

5. Jaggery/ Panela

Jaggery is commonly known as *gur* in India and panela in the rest of the world. Regular intake of jaggery in any form with any food will help combat anemia. Jaggery is unrefined sugar, in fact, it is the purest form of sugar and is prepared in iron vessels with fruit juices without any addition of synthetic chemicals. It is rich in iron and folate which help prevent anemia. Regular intake of jaggery with ginger juice helps in better absorption of iron.

6. Chickpeas

Chickpeas are Iron powerhouse for vegetarians. Chickpeas are high in fiber and protein and contain several key vitamins and minerals.

They are rich in iron, folate and vitamin C, which are necessary for the synthesis of hemoglobin. Higher protein and iron content of chickpeas, make them a smart option for vegetarians. Add lemon juice to hummus for better iron absorption.

7. Pumpkin Seeds

Pumpkin seeds are rich in iron, antioxidants, zinc, magnesium and many other nutrients.

Only a handful of pumpkin seeds every two days can help strengthen the immune system, prevent anemia. Add the roasted pumpkin seeds to morning cereal, bread, yogurt, or salad topping.

8. Fenugreek

The fenugreek seeds rich in proteins with essential amino acids, Iron, Ascorbate and Folate content, have restorative and nutritive properties. Fenugreek helps to prevent and cure anemia and maintain a good healthy life for a longer duration. The leaves of fenugreek help in blood formation. The seeds of fenugreek are also a valuable cure for anemia being rich in iron.

9. Soybeans

Soybeans are a major source of non-heme iron. Soybean is low in fat and high in protein and fiber that fights anemia. They're an excellent source of important minerals like copper, which helps keep our blood vessels and immune system healthy. It is also high in manganese, an essential nutrient involved in many chemical processes in the body.

10. Sesame Seeds

The iron in sesame seeds can keep the immune system functioning properly and prevent iron-deficient anemia. Especially the black sesame seeds are a rich source of iron. The seeds are packed with essential nutrients, like copper, phosphorus, vitamin E, and zinc as well. One quarter cup size serving of sesame seeds can provide 30% of the daily iron requirement.

Conclusion

Body cannot produce iron on its own which is an important mineral, it plays a key role in cell growth and differentiation, therefore, consuming Iron rich diet on a regular basis is important. Remember to include a source of vitamin C when eating non-heme plant sources of iron to boost its absorption in the body. Girls should increase iron consumption during periods to combat the blood loss, similarly women who are pregnant should increase the iron consumption as they are at a higher risk for developing anemia due to the excess amount of blood the body produces to help provide nutrients for the baby.

10. TOP 10 FOODS FOR VEGETARIANS TO PREVENT VITAMIN B12 DEFICIENCY

Top 10 Foods for Vegetarians to Prevent Vitamin B12 Deficiency

If you feel fatigued, depressed and irritated all the time, if you hear a ringing sound in 1 or both ears or experiencing memory trouble and poor balance then you may have Vitamin B12 Deficiency also known as Cobalamin Deficiency. Protein foods are the primary sources of vitamin B12, which include animal meats and fish this is why vegetarians often have a vitamin B12 deficiency.

What is Vitamin B12 and why it is important?

Vitamin B12, also known as cobalamin, is a water-soluble vitamin. It is an essential nutrient important in the normal functioning of the nervous system and keeps blood cells healthy and helps make DNA, the genetic material in human cells. Vitamin B12 deficiency may lead to a reduction in healthy red blood cells which may result in anemia. The Dietary Reference Intake (DRI), for adult men and women, is 2.4 micrograms of vitamin B12 in a day. Like other essential nutrients, Vitamin B12 can't be made by the body. Instead, it must be gotten from food.

If your vitamin B12 level is quite low then you have to take supplements or Vitamin B12 injections whichever is advised by your physician. But if you have borderline vitamin B12 deficiency or you want to prevent it in future then you must start eating Vitamin B12 rich food. Though Vitamin B12 is mainly found in animal sources, there are some vegetarian options to prevent its deficiency.

I am listing below the top 10 vitamin B12 rich foods for vegetarians.

1. Yogurt

Eating yogurt regularly is an excellent way to get more vitamin B12 into your diet. Yogurt, have the highest absorption of vitamin B12, between 50% and 75%. Yogurt is also a good source of folate and vitamin B6. Go for low fat, unsweetened plain yogurt to avoid weight gain.

2. Cow's Milk

Milk is another great food source of vitamin B12, and adequate consumption may aid in the prevention of vitamin B12 deficiency. About 2 cups of 250 ml of milk per day can get you the recommended daily intake of vitamin B12. It is loaded with other nutrients such as calcium, protein, potassium, and, phosphorus. Have it with breakfast cereal and you will get more Vitamin B12.

3. Cheese

Cheese is an excellent source of vitamin B12. Some types of cheese such as Swiss Cheese, Mozzarella cheese, and Cottage Cheese are high in vitamin B12, avoid processed cheese as the amount of vitamin B12 is very low in it. 1 slice of cheese is enough to provide you 22% to 36% of the recommended daily intake of vitamin B12 but don't solely depend upon cheese to fulfill your daily vitamin B12 requirement as large consumption of cheese may make you fat.

4. Soy Milk

As such soy milk doesn't naturally contain Vitamin B12, but it can be fortified with it. Fortified food means that has nutrients added to it that don't naturally occur in the food. In the case of soy milk, it is often fortified with Vitamin B12 - be sure to check the label. Avoid flavored ones and choose unsweetened varieties as they are more natural and free of void calories that is sugar. With just one cup of fortified soy milk, you can get a day's worth of vitamin B12 (2.4 micrograms).

5. Tempeh

Tempeh is made by a natural culturing and controlled fermentation process that binds soybeans into a cake form. Bacterial contamination during tempeh production may contribute to the increased Vitamin B12 content of tempeh. Amount of vitamin B12 present in tempeh is quite low in comparison to milk products, therefore you shouldn't solely rely on it to meet your daily recommended vitamin B12 requirement, but it can boost plant-based protein intake that gives you plenty of fiber with no cholesterol or saturated fat.

6. Dried Shiitake mushroom

Dried Shiitake Mushrooms, a type of fungi, have been shown to contain significant levels of B12. These are not an excellent source of vitamin B12 but something is better than nothing, you can increase your overall vitamin B12 intake by mixing dried shiitake mushrooms, tempeh, and cheese in your wraps and stuffing.

7. Whey Protein

Whey protein is a great source of vitamin B12. You can make your own whey protein at home by curdling boiled milk with lemon juice. The liquid part of this process is your whey which is not only rich in vitamin B12 but also a great source of protein for vegetarians. Use this whey in your pancake batter or add it in your pasta recipes to get full health benefits of whey.

8. Cereal

Breakfast cereal such as Muesli and Granola are a good source of vitamin B12. If you don't enjoy your cereal with milk then eat them as a snack during office break time or try as a late-night snack. Be sure to go for unsweetened varieties to avoid unnecessary fat in your diet.

9. Vanilla Ice Cream

Ice Cream is made of milk and Vitamin B12 is naturally found in milk, so that makes ice cream a good source Vitamin B12. Not only this, ice cream also contains vitamin A, B complex, C, D, K and E, calcium and protein. On the other hand, it is high in cholesterol and saturated fat, therefore, it should be consumed in lesser amount for overall health. A Single cup serving of vanilla ice cream contains 20 percent of the recommended daily intake of vitamin B12.

10. Rice Milk

Rice milk is a great source of vitamin B12. It has zero saturated fat and rich in vitamin A, D, calcium, magnesium, potassium, and iron. You can make it at your home by finely blending a ½ cup of cooked brown rice with 2 cups of water. For extra smooth rice milk, simply pass the liquid through the strainer to remove any lumps, it tastes best when served chilled.

Conclusion

Vitamin B12 Deficiency is not very uncommon in vegetarians but all is needed to do a little change in diet or more precisely just needed to add more vitamin B12 rich food in your diet. With some simple changes, you may have great results. Not only it will prevent you from vitamin B12 deficiency but it will also prevent you from anemia and as vitamin B12 foods are rich in protein, you will get double benefit with a healthy nervous system, healthy skin and many more.

ABOUT THE AUTHOR

La Fonceur is a dance artist, a health blogger and the author of the book series *Eat So What* and *Secret of Healthy Hair*. She has a master's degree in Pharmacy, and she is specialized in Pharmaceutical Technology. She has published a review article titled 'Techniques for Producing Biotechnology-Derived Products of Pharmaceutical Use' in Pharmtechmedica Journal. She is a registered state pharmacist. She is a national-level GPAT qualifier of the year 2011 in which she was among the top 1400 nationwide. Being a research scientist, she has worked closely with drugs. Based on her experience, she believes vegetarian foods are the remedy for many diseases; one can prevent most of the diseases with nutritional foods and a healthy lifestyle.

Note from La Fonceur

I am glad to find someone who is as health-conscious as much as I am. Being a Lacto Vegetarian, I always look for healthy vegetarian options to include in my diet. I hope this book has helped you gain deep knowledge of the foods that you eat and has provided you the guidance on how you can be healthy and disease-free just by adding correct foods in your diet that enhance your health and help fight diseases.

Please leave a review on your favorite platform if you have found my book helpful, it will encourage me to write more health books.

Also, if you are looking for a permanent solution to your hair problems you can read my book *Secret of Healthy Hair*. The book basically explains how can you influence your hair's health and its growth rate? How can you get the smooth, shiny, and strong hair that you always dreamt about? Additionally, this book includes some healthy recipes which promote hair growth along with a customized diet and lifestyle plan for every season.

Secret of Healthy Hair is available in paperback, hardcover, and eBook edition in all leading bookstores as well as online platforms.

La Fonceur

ALL BOOKS BY LA FONCEUR

Full versions:

Mini extract editions:

CONNECT WITH LA FONCEUR

Instagram: @la_fonceur | @eatsowhat

Facebook: LaFonceur | eatsowhat

Twitter: @la_fonceur

Amazon Author Page:

www.amazon.com/La-Fonceur/e/B07PM8SBSG/

Bookbub Author Page: www.bookbub.com/authors/la-fonceur

Sign up to website to get exclusive offers on La Fonceur eBooks:

Health Blog: www.eatsowhat.com

Website: www.lafonceur.com/sign-up

Lightning Source UK Ltd.
Milton Keynes UK
UKHW020703190520
363466UK00009B/314